HOW TO PASS

THE FIREFIGHTER SELECTION PROCESS

HOW TO PASS
THE FIREFIGHTER SELECTION PROCESS

Mike Bryon

KOGAN
PAGE

Publisher's note

Every possible effort has been made to ensure that the information contained in this book is accurate at the time of going to press, and the publishers and authors cannot accept responsibility for any errors or omissions, however caused. No responsibility for loss or damage occasioned to any person acting, or refraining from action, as a result of the material in this publication can be accepted by the editor, the publisher or any of the authors.

First published in Great Britain in 2004
Reprinted in 2005

Kogan Page Limited
120 Pentonville Road
London N1 9JN
United Kingdom
www.kogan-page.co.uk

British Library Cataloguing in Publication Data

A CIP record for this book is available from the British Library.

ISBN 0 7494 4244 1

Typeset by Saxon Graphics Ltd, Derby
Printed and bound in Great Britain by Creative Print and Design (Wales), Ebbw Vale

Contents

Acknowledgements

I owe thanks to the candidates who have attended the applicant firefighter courses on which I have taught. They showed such incredible commitment and determination to succeed in their desire to become a firefighter. If any failed a stage of the recruitment process then I was always impressed that they found the strength of character to apply again. Most of them are now serving firefighters and I wish them every success in their chosen career.

The practice questions are intended only as a means to prepare for the real tests and interview and the information contained should not be used for any other purpose. If a passage is on the subject of fire or fire safety then please remember that it has been written for the purposes of practice only and under no circumstances should it be relied on as a source of advice on how to prevent or fight fire.

The views expressed are not those of any of the Fire Authorities or any serving Firefighter or Officer but are drawn from my experience of helping applicant firefighters through the recruitment process. They and any errors therefore are entirely my own.

A career as a firefighter

The aim of this book is to help you prepare for the firefighter selection process.

On average there are 40 applicants for every firefighter position. When a Fire Authority advertises firefighter vacancies it is not uncommon for them to receive thousands of applications and they must select from these thousands in as fair a way as possible the successful candidates. It is no easy task and it involves choosing just a few from a great many very good candidates. The recruitment process is long, it can easily last six months, and is both physically and mentally demanding.

To succeed in becoming a firefighter will require you to make a major commitment in terms of time spent preparing for each stage of the recruitment process. Only then are you likely to demonstrate your full potential and address any areas of weakness. It may well involve the biggest commitment you have made in your life so far. If this sounds a bit of an exaggeration then remember that you will be one of many really determined candidates and some of them will have made a major commitment so if you do not do the same you are likely to come a poor second. Physically you will need to be very fit. You will need to think carefully about how you describe your approach to others. You should undertake some form of voluntary work. Spend hours practising written tests and address any areas of weakness in maths or English through further education if necessary. Prepare thoroughly for the interview and research into the Fire Service, the community you are to serve and the role of a firefighter. Do all this and you will vastly improve your chances of success.

There are many people who really want to become firefighters and who have applied and failed repeatedly. If you are such a person then you will recognize the sense of rejection and disappointment felt when your latest application fails. You will also have shown considerable determination and courage to try once again in the face of such rejection.

Having your application rejected does not mean that you could not be a successful firefighter. In fact most successful applicants have previously failed; in some cases candidates only succeed after applying for years and after 5 or more applications. So if you are sure it is what you want and the reason for your disappointment is not due to a medical condition or disability then keep going, keep seeking to improve yourself and push aside feelings of self-doubt or resentment.

I have trained both men and women applicant firefighters and helped them prepare for each stage of the recruitment process used by the particular Authorities at that time. I trust that this book is a far better source of help and advice as a result of the time I spent with these applicants and I am indebted to them. May I take this opportunity to wish them continued success and to wish you every success in your efforts also to join the service.

The role of the firefighter and key responsibilities

It is common to think of firefighters as heroes who save the lives of people in danger from fire, road accident or flood. Accounts of their bravery are regularly reported in our newspapers and a great many people are extremely grateful for the life-saving help they have provided. However, the drama and action of an emergency are but one part of the firefighter's role and to do well in the recruitment process you must be able to demonstrate an understanding of the many essential duties that are a part of the job.

The Authority to which you apply will send you details which may well include an account of the role of firefighter; this document is something you should study carefully and reflect upon. It may include the following responsibilities:

1. Working in the community to promote fire safety.
2. Constantly developing your understanding of the community that you serve.
3. A commitment and understanding of equality and valuing diversity.
4. A commitment to maintain your knowledge, skills and fitness throughout your career.
5. Integrity when dealing with colleagues and the public.
6. Dependability to see a job through.
7. Working as a part of a team to solve problems and resolve emergencies.
8. Supporting colleagues.
9. Communicating fire safety to all sections of the public, including members of challenging sections of our community.
10. Working in difficult conditions, confined spaces, heights, dirt and heat or cold and wet.
11. Sharing accommodation.
12. Working at unsocial times and on shifts.
13. Facing distressing and pressurized situations.
14. Dealing sympathetically with people who are perhaps emotional and distressed.

Background reading

A very informative source of information about the service and its future organization is the White Paper entitled 'Our Fire and Rescue Service' presented to Parliament by the Deputy Prime Minister in June 2003.

The paper sets out the government's plans to reform the Fire Service. The intention is to update procedures, practice and laws, some of which date back 50 years. The changes include a greater emphasis on the prevention of fire and more partnership working with the community it serves. The paper stresses how important the Service has become since 9/11 and extends the role of the service to help meet the growing threat of, for example, chemical or biological attack.

You can read the paper on www.odpm.gov.uk; click on 'fire'. This site also has a worthwhile newsletter about the service.

Experience

There is no particular prior experience that qualifies you to be a firefighter. Almost any past is acceptable so long as you can present it in interview and on the application form in terms that show you demonstrate the qualities and responsibilities relevant to the service.

You may be asked, for example, to describe an occasion when you had to solve a problem. Your answer can be drawn from any aspect of your past, including time in the home raising a family, at school, college or work.

Some Fire Authorities are making it a requirement of all applicants that they hold a full UK driving licence (they may allow you to apply if you are learning to drive but your future appointment will depend on you gaining a licence).

The application forms

All Fire Authorities will require you to complete a set of application forms and some may require you to complete initial and supplementary forms as you progress through the selection process.

Getting hold of a set of forms may be harder than you expect and this may represent your first of many challenges. Obtaining a set of forms may prove a challenge because in some instances so many candidates register an interest that the Authority feels obliged to limit the number of forms sent out. They may do this by, for example, issuing applications on a first come first served basis until the agreed number is reached. So register your interest straight way. Alternatively, they may issue applications only to applicants selected randomly by computer from the total list of all initial applicants.

If you receive an application form, look after it! If you lose it or spill coffee over it you are unlikely to be offered a replacement. It may well comprise more than one part and you will be required to complete and return all sections. So get one or more photocopies of the blank forms and put the original away in a safe place. Write your answers on to the photocopied forms and only when you are completely happy with all your responses and you have carefully checked your answers write out your answers on to the real forms.

Make a note of the closing date by when the completed forms must be submitted and read carefully and keep all the information sent with it. Make sure you complete the forms using a black pen if that is what the instructions require and complete them in very neat handwriting with no spelling mistakes. Only submit the original forms as photocopies are unlikely to be accepted.

Most candidates spend far too little time on the application forms; they fail to give proper consideration to the questions and do not think carefully enough about their answer. Take the application forms very seriously – they may well represent the stage when most applicants are rejected. It is likely that, for example, 3,000 application forms are issued and only a thousand or so returned forms will be accepted and those applicants invited to the next stage of the process. The rest will be rejected on the grounds that the information provided did not meet the criteria of the Fire Authority.

You application will be judged by what you write in response to the questions and the accuracy with which you complete the forms. You must answer every question and what you state must be truthful, relevant and clear.

Take a copy of your completed forms and keep it for future reference. You might be asked about your answers at the interview stage and you may, for example, be asked to explain what you meant or to provide further information.

Tips on completing the questions

The forms may comprise any or all of three styles of question and you need to approach each type differently. They are:

Question type 1. These are requests for straightforward personal details such as your name, date of birth, medical history, qualifications that you hold, details of any criminal convictions and so on.

The Authority needs this information so that they can contact you and monitor the recruitment process to establish that it is reaching all sections of the community. They also want to establish that you qualify under the basic criteria for being a firefighter. They should have provided you with details of these basic criteria. They include, for example, an age criterion and minimal level of medical health which are considered essential if you are to be a firefighter. They may also require you to hold a driving licence. Take care to reread the details provided and satisfy yourself that you meet all the requirements.

Make sure that you provide accurately all the information requested. If you overlook one of the questions then the Authority may have no alternative but to reject your application as they are unable to establish whether or not you fulfil the basic criteria for the position.

Many of the details that you provide are checked at a later stage in the process. You will, for example, attend a medical, and a police check will be undertaken to confirm that you do not have certain types of criminal convictions. So do not be tempted to omit any information that you feel might count against you. If you are worried about disclosing something then call the recruitment section of the Fire Authority and ask for further guidance.

Question type 2. These provide you with an opportunity to describe things that you have done or are interested in that best demonstrate your suitability for the position of firefighter.

This sort of question typically provides a space on the form and requires you to write a brief statement (say, 50–70 words) in answer to a question. Example questions may include some of the following issues:

1. Describe when you have worked as a part of a team.

2. Detail any voluntary or community work that you have undertaken.

[ ]

3. Briefly describe a situation when you have had to share sleeping facilities.

[ ]

4. Explain when you have worked together with others to solve a practical problem.

[ ]

5. Describe a situation when you have undertaken tasks in very hot, cramped or dirty conditions.

[ ]

6. How would you describe the community in which you live?

[ ]

7. Describe how you have dealt with a stressful situation.

[ ]

8. Explain when you have shown commitment.

```
┌─────────────────────────────────────────────────────────┐
│                                                           │
│                                                           │
│                                                           │
└─────────────────────────────────────────────────────────┘
```

9. Detail any training that you have undertaken.

```
┌─────────────────────────────────────────────────────────┐
│                                                           │
│                                                           │
│                                                           │
└─────────────────────────────────────────────────────────┘
```

10. Describe how you keep yourself physically fit.

```
┌─────────────────────────────────────────────────────────┐
│                                                           │
│                                                           │
│                                                           │
└─────────────────────────────────────────────────────────┘
```

Take your time over this type of question. You will not come up with the best answers on your first attempt. Think carefully about the question and how it relates to the role of a firefighter. Try to make every word count.

When answering this type of question you can refer to experiences from any sphere of your life and not just work, college or school. In fact, it may well be best if you include in at least one of your answers a relevant experience from an interest that you have or one that has arisen within your family or circle of friends. Avoid using the same example to make a variety of points.

Make sure that you have an answer to every question and use up all the space provided. Be sure that what you write is relevant to the question. Think of more than one experience that you could use and then decide which one best answers the question. Test your answer out on friends or family and encourage them to suggest things that you have done that you might use.

There is no need to exaggerate your past or invent things. Lots of everyday, ordinary experiences demonstrate that you have the experience, skills and knowledge to perform the role of firefighter.

Check to ensure that your answer forms a proper series of sentences and reads well.

Practise on the example questions above and you will find that thinking about these issues may also help you prepare for an interview.

Question type 3. With this type you indicate how you are likely to respond to a number of situations or what your approach would be to the demands of the job of firefighter.

This type of question usually requires a multiple choice response where you indicate if you agree or disagree with a statement or indicate whether or not you have experience of something.

To give you a flavour of this sort of question, examples might include:

1. Is honesty always the best policy?
2. I enjoy manual labour.
3. Firefighting is more important than fire prevention.
4. I am happiest when working in an office.
5. If you know you are right about something then the views of others must be wrong.
6. My work sometimes involves me explaining things to groups of people.
7. I am the sort of person who gets more done working on my own than as a part of a team.
8. It is better to help a neighbour than a stranger.
9. At work I prefer to give orders than receive them.
10. If your superior tells you to do something then you should do it no matter what you think.
11. The fire station cannot be a part of the local community in the same way as the school or hospital.
12. I can speak a second language fluently.

13. I agree that actions speak louder than words.
14. I have recently undertaken work that involves wearing a uniform.
15. A person who cannot speak English cannot expect to get the same service as someone who can.
16. I have considerable experience in operating heavy plant and machinery.
17. Being strong is more important to a firefighter than local knowledge.
18. I have never told a lie in my life.
19. I have worked at nights, weekends and on public holidays.
20. If someone is annoying me I would keep it to myself.
21. I know the name of my neighbour and speak to them regularly.
22. I like always to be doing things and get restless if I sit around.
23. I sometimes work at heights.
24. It is best not to upset people by telling them something they do not want to hear.
25. I'm not the sort of person who worries about taking risks.

To these questions you are required to indicate whether or not you agree or disagree with the statement or whether or not it is a true statement about you. You may be asked if you agree or disagree strongly or only partially with the statement.

I have not provided answers to these example questions as your response would depend on your views and experiences and not mine. It is important that you take time over these questions. Think them through before you decide on your answer. You should always answer the questions truthfully and remember the context of the question. You are applying to become a firefighter and it is in this context that you are answering the question. Forget about getting too philosophical or deeply into the issue and ask yourself as an applicant firefighter: 'What is my answer to that question or statement?'

Take the first example question, 'Is honesty always the best policy?' You should be able to answer this question truthfully and positively. You might be able to think up some unlikely situation where being dishonest could be the best thing to do, say to protect someone you love, a child perhaps, from what might be a very hurtful situation and for this reason you might conclude that no, honesty is not always the best policy. However, think about the question from the point of view of the Fire Service, who do not want dishonest firefighters. The unlikely situation would not apply to you in the role of firefighter and a firefighter is placed into a position of high trust by the general public. Dishonesty in a firefighter would never be the best policy.

Responding truthfully will sometimes mean that you admit to something that appears to count against you succeeding in your application. For example, if you do not speak a second language fluently or if you have never worn a uniform at work then you must be prepared to say so. It is unlikely that a few of these answers will exclude you from the next state and anyway if you lie and it is discovered at interview your application will be rejected at that later stage.

What to do if your application is rejected

Contact the Fire Authority to which you have applied and request that they explain to you why your application failed. Take a careful note of what they say and write it down so that you can reflect on it later.

Refer back to your copy of your application and the notes that the Authority sent to you originally. Reread both and try to identify where your application could be improved. Ask a friend or relative to look at your forms and make suggestions on how they think the forms might be improved.

Consider beginning some voluntary work in your community or offer to help an elderly neighbour with his or her garden or home maintenance. This way you may be able to gain valuable experience and answer more of the questions positively. Visit your local fire station, tell them of your wish to become a fire-fighter and ask them if they are willing to show you around the station. When on the visit ask the firefighters how they think you might be able to improve your prospects.

Research on the Web the responsibilities and priorities of the Fire Service and think about your answers to the questions in the context of what is important to the Service. Find out about the Service's commitment to equality of opportunity both amongst its staff and in the provision of services to the general public. Think about how such a commitment can be delivered on a day-to-day basis by firefighters and possibly reconsider some of your answers in the light of the Service's commitment to equality. Read about the Service's efforts to improve the public's knowledge of fire prevention as well as firefighting and see if you should reconsider any of your answers in the light of this information. Visit your local library and find out more about the community in which you live and the services offered to the young and old and the socially excluded. Research the ethnic minority groups that live in your community, the minority religions and languages spoken. Apply again as soon as you can.

Written tests and practice questions

The recruitment process to become a firefighter is almost certain to include a set of psychometric tests. After the sift of application forms these tests represent the next greatest challenge in your quest to become a firefighter.

It may be that you are required to undertake a physical fitness test on the same day as the written tests. If this is the case, be sure that you are training both mentally and physically in preparation for what will be a very important day. See Chapter 5 for advice on any physical test.

Practice can make the difference between pass and fail in the written tests. This chapter comprises hundreds of practice questions relevant to the main types of test used by fire authorities to select firefighters. Answers and many explanations are provided in Chapter 6.

The authority to which you applied should have sent you an invitation to attend for the test and a description of the type of questions and format of the test that you face. If they have not done this then have a look on their Web site to see if they describe the test there or consider telephoning and asking them to describe to you the tests that they use.

Select from this chapter the practice questions that are most similar to the type of question in the real test that you face and restrict your practice to these questions. Additional practice material might be found in other Kogan Page publications. See 'sources of further information and practice' for titles.

The types of written test in use

The written test is likely to comprise a series of sub-tests that will be administrated one after the other with a short pause between each.

Sub-tests may be multiple choice where you have to select one answer as correct from a number of suggestions or short answer tests where you have to write an answer in an answer box.

Some tests may require you to listen to a taped message or watch a video and then answer questions against a time limit. Other tests will comprise a test booklet that contains questions that you must read or interpret before answering questions.

Typical examples of sub-tests used for the recruitment of fire-fighters are: understanding information, understanding audio passages, verbal reasoning, using numbers, numerical reasoning, non-verbal reasoning, spatial reasoning and obser-vation.

This title provides practice material or advice on all these types of sub-test.

How practice can help

You must seek to achieve the very best score possible in the written tests. Every point counts and two things will help you do this. First, realize that practice prior to the test will help you to become familiar with the test's demands, build up speed and accuracy, avoid common mistakes and deal with any nervousness. If passing is important to you then you should be prepared to make a major commitment in terms of setting time aside to practise. Second, realize that doing well in a test is not simply down to intelligence but also requires you to be determined to do well and to try very hard. When the test administrator says 'Stop! Please put your pencils down', you should feel exhausted as a result of the mental effort you have made. Otherwise you risk not doing yourself justice.

Practice will mean the difference between pass and fail for some candidates. However, if you have never got on with maths or if your reading skills are not what they could be then the practice contained here may not be sufficient. If you have difficulties with your numeracy or literacy and are determined to become a firefighter then get yourself along to a college of further education or some other institution and enrol on a foundation or literacy or numeracy course. It really could make all the difference. Once you have completed the course, use the material in this book to press home your advantage and maximize your test score. When you have passed the written test and are invited for interview, don't forget to mention the fact that you were so committed to become a firefighter that you went to college to improve yourself. It will be a credit to you.

If you suffer from a learning disability such as dyslexia and have been formally assessed by an educational psychologist then you may be allowed extra time in which to complete the written test. Contact the Authority straight away and ask them if they are able to accommodate your disability.

To maximize the benefits of practice you should be prepared to practise for a minimum of 20 hours over the weeks leading up to your test. If you can obtain sufficient material and can commit the time then feel free to practise a lot more than this. But remember that if you are really weak at maths or English then be prepared to make a major commitment over months. Undertake two sorts of practice:

Practice type 1

Work on realistic practice questions from this chapter in a relaxed situation without time constraint. The aim of this practice is to get used to the style of question, to realize what the skills are that are being examined and relearn them; if you get questions wrong, go over them and understand why you are getting them wrong. Use this time to recognize what you need to do better in order to improve your performance in the test. Focus most of your time on what you are least good at.

Practice type 2

Once you feel confident in each of the types of question that you face in the real firefighter test, start practising on realistic questions under strict time constraints and under exam-type conditions. You will find five realistic practice tests in Chapter 4. The aim of this second sort of practice is to get used to answering questions under the pressure of time and to build up your speed and accuracy in answering questions when under pressure. By all means make up more practice tests by selecting practice questions from this chapter and setting a time limit. If you can, get someone to act as a test administrator to read out the instructions, tell you when to begin and when to stop when you have run out of time. Help from someone is really essential for practice in any test where you have to listen to a passage and then answer questions.

On the day of the test

To understand what it will be like on the day, think back to the exams at school. You are invited to attend a training or recruitment centre at a particular time – do not be even a minute late and dress smartly. You are likely to be one of many candidates invited that day. If you are to undertake a physical test as well as the written test then you will need to bring a change of sports clothes and training shoes and you may well need to attend the centre for most of the day. All this detail will be included in your letter of invitation so read it carefully.

It is really important that you listen carefully to the instructions provided before the test begins. You may feel nervous and this may affect your concentration so make yourself focus on what is being said. Much of what you will be told will be a repeat of the information provided in the test description sent to you with the letter inviting you to the test. So read and reread this document before the day of the test.

Pay particular attention to instructions detailing how many questions there are in each sub-test and then during the test make sure that you have answered all the questions. I have seen candidates who have failed to turn over the page during a test and so fail to answer all the questions. Had they listened to the instructions more carefully then they would have answered all 30 questions rather than reaching the bottom of the page and deciding that the test must be over when they have only answered 10 questions.

It is important to organize your time before the test, and it is even more essential that you keep track of time during the test and manage how long you spend on any one question. You must keep going right up to the end. If it is applicable, take the last few minutes to go over the questions checking your work. This is where the practice at mock exams under strict time limits really helps.

You should aim to get right the balance between speed and accuracy. To do well you must work quickly whilst making the minimum of mistakes.

Everyone gets some answers wrong. It is better that you risk getting some questions wrong but attempt every question rather than double-check every answer and be told that you have run out of time before you have finished all the questions.

When you hit a difficult section or question don't lose heart. Just keep going – you may well find that you come next to a section or question in which you can excel.

If you do not know an answer then educated guessing is worth while and worth practising. If you are unsure of an answer to a multiple choice question, consider all the suggested answers and try ruling some out as wrong. This way you can reduce the number of suggested answers from which to guess and hopefully increase your chances of guessing correctly.

Make sure that you adopt the right approach during the test. The candidates that do best are the ones who look forward to the challenge of a test and the opportunity to demonstrate their abilities. They realize that they have nothing to lose if they do their best and 'go for it'. It is critical that you approach the test with confidence in your own abilities, and preparation is the key to confidence.

What to do if you fail

It is likely that over half of the candidates will fail. If you are one of those who do not pass then understand that it does not mean that you do not have the potential to be a firefighter. Ask the Authority to provide you with feedback on your score and identify which part of the test you had a problem with. Recall and note down the types of question and the level of difficulty that they represented. Be honest with yourself and try to assess what it is you need to do in order to pass the next time. I know firefighters who repeatedly failed the written tests. For some of them it was only when they set about a major programme of improving their maths or English or both that they then went on to pass. Others simply needed to get more used to the test and working under the pressure of time in an exam-type situation.

To reapply you will have to wait for another recruitment round and resubmit another application form, and assuming that you pass the application form sift then you will be called again for the test. In the meantime plan a programme of revision and improvement and work hard on the areas in which you were weakest last time. Do not forget to maintain your programme of physical fitness training at the same time.

It will take courage and determination to try again and to keep working to improve yourself until you pass. But courage and determination are exactly the qualities that a firefighter is expected to demonstrate. So decide if you are prepared to make the necessary commitment and, if you are, and you go on to succeed, then it will be something of which you can be rightly proud.

Practice questions

In the remainder of this chapter you will find hundreds of practice questions in seven types of question relevant to the firefighter practice test. Some of the questions are intended to help you to develop the skills tested by the real test. These questions may therefore be easier than the real questions but for some candidates they are essential preparation and will help you to achieve the confidence and speed demanded by the real test. If you are sure you already have these skills then feel free to skip these sections. Further question types are covered in Chapter 5.

Understanding information

In this type of test your task is to read a passage and answer a series of questions. Each question comprises a statement about the passage and you must indicate if the statement is true, false, or you cannot tell whether it is true or false. You make your decision based only on the information contained in the passage.

This sort of question may seem straightforward in that you can always refer back to the passage to answer each question.

However, these tests are done under tight time constraints and such an approach may mean that you run out of time before you have attempted all the questions. The best approach requires just one, fast, very attentive reading of the passage before answering the questions and perhaps going back to the passage on only a few occasions.

It is really important that you do not bring to the question knowledge or information not contained in the passage. You should resist answering the question on the basis of any information other than that contained in the passage even if it is on a subject of which you know a great deal.

For example, the passage says 'pigs can fly' and the question asks 'can pigs fly?' Even though we all know pigs cannot fly the correct answer is true. Equally, if the passage makes no reference to whether or not pigs can fly then the answer to the question would be 'cannot tell'.

With practice you can much improve in this type of question. Try the following 50 questions, which are all on Fire Service-related subjects, and seek to build up your speed and confidence. Answers and many explanations are provided on pages 193–198.

Important note
Please note that the passages are made up for the purpose of providing realistic practice only and in many respects may be factually incorrect. The passages should not be relied on as a source of information on the subject of fire prevention or fire-fighting, nor do they necessarily describe correctly how you should act in any of the situations described.

Passage 1

Dressed in a firefighter's protective suit, boots and helmet and holding no more than a fire blanket, I entered the blackened room to face a flaming pan on a cooker. The heat and smoke were increasing by the second. I guarded my hands with the blanket and held it up high, remembering my training that the blanket had to be above the flames and should never be thrown. I advanced carefully, slowly, to avoid a slip or trip that could prove fatal. I draped the blanket over the blazing chip pan. Immediately the blanket was sucked into the container by the flames creating a vacuum as they fought for oxygen and the fire was out.

I had attended a day of theory in fire prevention and fire-fighting at the Maritime Safety Centre in Gosport. I learnt that a fire aboard a ship was most likely to happen because of poorly maintained electrical equipment and oil or grease left to accumulate around hot engines. On the second day of the course we put into practice what we had been taught.

Questions

Q1.   The trainee firefighter was wearing everyday street clothes.

True
False
Cannot say

Answer

Q2.   The fire was aboard a ship.

True
False
Cannot say

Answer

Q3.   The thing on fire was a chip pan.

    True
    False
    Cannot say

    Answer [   ]

Q4.   The fire blanket was sucked into the pan before the flames died.

    True
    False
    Cannot say

    Answer [   ]

Q5.   The training centre was in Southampton.

    True
    False
    Cannot say

    Answer [   ]

Q6.   Oil and grease cause most fires on ships.

    True
    False
    Cannot say

    Answer [   ]

Q7.   The course covered both firefighting and fire prevention.

    True
    False
    Cannot say

    Answer [   ]

Q8.   Chip pans should not be used on board a boat.

True
False
Cannot say

Answer ▢

Q9.   The trainee was taught to walk slowly to avoid a trip.

True
False
Cannot say

Answer ▢

Q10.   You have to be physically and mentally fit to fight a fire.

True
False
Cannot say

Answer ▢

Passage 2

Holding a cup of water fixed to a very long pole the instructor carefully poured the water into the relit pan of burning oil which by this stage was very hot. Suddenly, there was an explosion and a ball of flames hit the roof of the room and rapidly rolled out across the whole room. The speed and intensity of the reaction was shocking and frightening. The instructor had deliberately made the potentially lethal error of trying to put out a class B fire (a burning liquid) with water. We had been told that the flame could move at 5 metres per second and was fuelled by droplets of burning oil carried by steam.

Another fire risk on ships is aerosol cans which are used to hold so many things such as furniture polish, kitchen cleaner, fly killer, oil and so on. On a boat there are often many of these cans and if a fire occurs and one of these cans is consumed by the flames then there is a high risk that an explosion will occur.

Before the end of the second day of the course the instructor demonstrated the use of foam, carbon dioxide and dry powder extinguishers and ensured that each trainee had first-hand experience of each type. It was explained that the carbon dioxide extinguishers were pressurized vessels and so the heaviest, and that dry powder when set off created a great deal of white dust.

Q11. You are unlikely to find many aerosols on boats.

> True
> False
> Cannot say
>
> Answer [   ]

Q12. The trainee firefighters practised with a CO_2 and foam-filled extinguisher only.

> True
> False
> Cannot say
>
> Answer [   ]

Q13. The explosion happened because water was poured on to a burning liquid.

> True
> False
> Cannot say
>
> Answer [   ]

Q14. The passage states that the trainees witnessed two explosions.

True
False
Cannot say

Answer [   ]

Q15. The heaviest extinguishers are pressure vessels.

True
False
Cannot say

Answer [   ]

Q16. In the passage the trainees were warned that it is the smoke that kills you and not the flames.

True
False
Cannot say

Answer [   ]

Q17. The two-day course covered both the theory and practice of fire prevention.

True
False
Cannot say

Answer [   ]

Q18. A class B fire can be put out with a foam-filled extinguisher.

True
False
Cannot say

Answer [   ]

Q19. In 7 seconds the ball of flame caused by the burning oil exploding could travel further than 25 metres.

True
False
Cannot say

Answer [   ]

Q20. Foam extinguishers give off a white dust.

True
False
Cannot say

Answer [   ]

Passage 3

Under recent legislation every place of work should have a written fire emergency plan. It should be specific to the workplace and detail the procedure in place in the event of fire. The plan should comment on the action to be taken on the discovery of a fire, how staff are to warn others of the emergency, how the fire brigade are to be informed and how staff are to evacuate the building and where to assemble. The fire-fighting equipment provided must be identified and properly maintained. The plan should be regularly practised by all the staff involved and the alarm system tested weekly to ensure that it is functioning properly.

Q21. A fire emergency plan should detail actions taken on the discovery of a fire.

True
False
Cannot say

Answer [   ]

Q22. The passage states that fire-fighting equipment must be properly maintained.

True
False
Cannot say

Answer [   ]

Q23. The plan is to specify the procedure in the event of a fire.

True
False
Cannot say

Answer [   ]

Q24. The passage states that an alarm system must be fitted.

True
False
Cannot say

Answer [   ]

Q25. The point of this passage is to explain how to tackle an electrical fire at work.

True
False
Cannot say

Answer [   ]

Passage 4

Firefighting always comes second to the safety of yourself and others. The first action on discovering a fire should be to raise the alarm. This may mean shouting 'fire, fire!' followed by the operation of a fire alarm call point if there is one. Once the alarm has been raised circumstances will determine whether or not you should try to fight the fire. However, more important than fighting a fire is ensuring the evacuation of people. It is important to make sure that people do not use lifts or go back into a building. People should only attempt to fight a fire if they are trained to do so and it does not involve unacceptable risk.

Q26. Once you have raised the alarm the most important thing is to evacuate the people.

True
False
Cannot say

Answer [   ]

Q27. Disabled people should use the lifts in order that they may leave the building quickly.

True
False
Cannot say

Answer [   ]

Q28. People once evacuated should assemble at the designated locations.

True
False
Cannot say

Answer [   ]

Q29. The passage states that a fire warden should raise the alarm by shouting 'fire, fire!'

True
False
Cannot say

Answer [   ]

Q30. Firefighting is something you should consider after completing all the other tasks.

True
False
Cannot say

Answer [   ]

Passage 5

All workplaces should be provided with adequate equipment for fighting fires. However, only people trained in its use should attempt to operate it. When deciding which type of extinguisher to use it is important to take into account the type of fire involved. Before anyone starts to fight a fire they must make sure that they have a clear exit route. When tackling the fire they should always position themselves between the fire and the way out.

Water is used on class A fires which include solid materials. Foam can be used on type B and C fires which include fires that involve liquids (type B) and gases (type C). Carbon dioxide can be used on electrical fires. Dry powder can be used on most types of fire.

Q31. When fighting a fire your back will most likely be facing your exit.

True
False
Cannot say

Answer [   ]

Q32. A burning table would be an example of a class A fire.

True
False
Cannot say

Answer [   ]

Q33. A burning pan of oil could be extinguished with a foam-filled extinguisher.

True
False
Cannot say

Answer [   ]

Q34. The passage states that all homes should be provided with adequate firefighting equipment.

True
False
Cannot say

Answer [   ]

Q35. This passage explains the advantages of each type of extinguisher.

True
False
Cannot say

Answer

Passage 6

The greatest danger is the spread of fire, heat and smoke. If this happens, the main risk to people is from the smoke, which can quickly overcome them and prevent them from escaping. If there is no adequate means of escape or if a fire can become big before it is noticed, then people may become trapped or overcome by heat or smoke before they can evacuate. An assessment of the risk of fire should include the likely speed of growth and spread of any fire and the heat and smoke generated. It should also estimate the number of people that may be found in an area and describe how they are to become aware of a fire and how they will make their escape.

Q36. How quickly a fire might spread should be considered in an assessment of the risk of fire.

True
False
Cannot say

Answer

Q37. The passage states that if people become trapped then smoke and heat are the main threat as they can incapac- itate them.

True
False
Cannot say

Answer [   ]

Q38. Firefighting equipment and full training in its operation must be provided.

True
False
Cannot say

Answer [   ]

Q39. A smoke alarm would quickly raise the alarm in the event of a fire.

True
False
Cannot say

Answer [   ]

Q40. A workplace assessment should investigate how workers are to become aware of a fire.

True
False
Cannot say

Answer [   ]

Passage 7

For fire to occur there must be a source of ignition, fuel and oxygen. If all three are present then the risk of fire exists; if they are in close proximity then the risk of fire increases. Oxygen is present in the air; sometimes it is also present in chemical form. Ignition can come from naked flames, hot surfaces, friction caused by drive belts, electrical sparks from static electricity or switches. Fuel can be anything that burns, including textiles, wood, paper, plastics or furniture. Liquids, including petrol, paints, adhesives and gases such as acetylene, are also potential fuels.

A risk assessment should list the potential sources of ignition and fuels that are present and describe how a fire can be prevented.

Q41. The passage states that if a source of ignition, fuel and oxygen are all present then a fire will occur.

True
False
Cannot say

Answer

Q42. Oxygen is found only in the air.

True
False
Cannot say

Answer

Q43. The closer together a source of ignition, fuel and oxygen are, the greater the risk of a fire.

True
False
Cannot say

Answer [   ]

Q44. Acetylene is more inflammable than petrol.

True
False
Cannot say

Answer [   ]

Q45. This passage describes the conditions necessary for a fire to occur.

True
False
Cannot say

Answer [   ]

Passage 8

A fire risk assessment seeks to identify the risk of a fire occurring and the fire hazards that are present. A hazard is something that could cause harm, while risk is the chance of that hazard actually causing harm.

An assessment must be specific to a particular place and must be carried out by someone who understands basic fire safety principles and has knowledge relating to the particular place. A risk assessment should identify all the fire hazards and risks present in a location and then determine whether or not they are acceptable or whether further action is required to reduce the risk.

Q46. An assessment must be written by someone who knows the place to which an assessment relates.

True
False
Cannot say

Answer [   ]

Q47. If an assessment identifies unacceptable fire hazards then it should determine if further action should be taken in order to reduce those hazards.

True
False
Cannot say

Answer [   ]

Q48. The passage makes it clear that a naked flame and petrol represent a fire hazard.

True
False
Cannot say

Answer [   ]

Q49. Once the fire hazards and risks are identified then an assessment is complete.

True
False
Cannot say

Answer [   ]

Q50. The passage describes features of a fire risk assessment.

True
False
Cannot say

Answer [   ]

Verbal reasoning

This sort of test examines your understanding of the relation-ships between pairs of words. The relationship being examined may be words that have the same or similar meanings, words that are related or examples of the same sort of subject or topic or words that have opposite meanings.

Verbal reasoning tests can be organized in a variety of ways and the practice questions are offered in the two most common formats. Irrespective of how they are organized, they all examine your vocabulary and ability to identify the most appropriate word in a given situation.

With practice you can show a significant improvement in this sort of question. It also helps to use a thesaurus, which is a type of dictionary that groups words with similar meaning. Another important way to improve in these tests is to find time to read a quality newspaper or journals, making sure that you look up the meaning of any words whose meaning you do not know.

Verbal reasoning question type 1

In this type of question you are given two pairs of words but from one pair a word is missing. You must try to identify the relationship that exists between the complete pair. You must then choose from a list of words one that completes the pair with the same type of relationship as the first pair. Try the 25 examples, the first of which is completed.

Q1.   Boat   Sails
      Car   ?

      A   Engine
      B   Tyres
      C   Journeys
      D   Motorbikes

      Answer   ☐

Q1.   Answer A.

Explanation A boat can be powered by sails and a car by its engine.

Q2.   Fire   Smoke
      Words   ?

      A   Letters
      B   Sentences
      C   Voices
      D   Dictionary

      Answer   ☐

Q3.   Telephone   ?
      River   Sea

      A   Receiver
      B   Ring tone
      C   Conversation
      D   Exchange

      Answer   ☐

Q4. Surface   ?
     Fuzzy   Smooth
     A   Veneer
     B   Interior
     C   Appearance
     D   Horizontal

     Answer   ☐

Q5. Jailed   Fraud
     Expelled   ?
     A   School
     B   Smoking
     C   Kick off
     D   Child

     Answer   ☐

Q6. ?   Engineer
     Swan   Bird
     A   Mechanical
     B   Scientist
     C   Project
     D   Professional

     Answer   ☐

Q7. ?   Mushy
     Polish   Waxy
     A   Feeble
     B   Soup
     C   Baby food
     D   Sentimental

     Answer   ☐

Q8.   Height   Weight
      Joyous   ?
      A   Beautiful
      B   Attractive
      C   Sombre
      D   Occasion
      Answer   ☐

Q9.   Inflate   ?
      Guess   Estimate
      A   Magnify
      B   Deflate
      C   Solve
      D   Expand
      Answer   ☐

Q10. Sensible   Stupid
      Opaque   ?
      A   Cloudy
      B   Transparent
      C   Obscure
      D   Dumb
      Answer   ☐

Q11. Pages   Book
      ?   Cloth
      A   Yarns
      B   Cloths
      C   Fibre
      D   Yard
      Answer   ☐

Q12. ?   Key
      Violin   Bow
      A   Ship
      B   Arrow
      C   Musical note
      D   Lock

      Answer   ☐

Q13. Barley   Cereal
      Parliament   ?
      A   Election
      B   Democracy
      C   Assembly
      D   ´   Government

      Answer   ☐

Q14. Photosynthesis Sunlight
      ?   Concert
      A   Hall
      B   Symphony
      C   Orchestra
      D   Performance

      Answer   ☐

Q15. Acid   Alkali
      Lax   ?
      A   Slack
      B   Blame
      C   Strict
      D   Casual

      Answer   ☐

Q16. Microscope   ?

	Language	Communication
A		Exploration
B		Magnification
C		Population
D		Classification

Answer   ☐

Q17. ?   Crate

	Divide	Distribute
A		Disturbance
B		Vegetables
C		Chaos
D		Chest

Answer   ☐

Q18. Proponent   Supporter

	?	Myth
A		Hero
B		Sorcerer
C		Story
D		Truth

Answer   ☐

Q19. Painkiller   ?

	Hockey	Ballgame
A		Medicine
B		Cure
C		Compound
D		Sport

Answer   ☐

Q20. Natural   ?

     Convict   Acquit
     A   Wholesome
     B   Spoiled
     C   Virtuous
     D   Synthetic

     Answer   ☐

Q21. Geology   Science

     Statistics   ?
     A   Knowledge
     B   Mathematics
     C   Probability
     D   Business Studies

     Answer   ☐

Q22. Oblong   ?

     Set square   Ruler
     A   Circumference
     B   Chart
     C   Cuboid
     D   Hoop

     Answer   ☐

Q23. ?   Weaken

     Refuse   Decline
     A   Dilute
     B   Destroy
     C   Poorly
     D   Brittle

     Answer   ☐

Q24. Construction Transportation

      Turtle   ?

      A   Dove

      B   Bird

      C   Animal

      D   Lizard

      Answer   ☐

Q25. Flyover   Viaduct

      ?   Ayatollah

      A   Archbishop

      B   Islam

      C   Religion

      D   Prayers

      Answer   ☐

Verbal reasoning question type 2

This style of verbal reasoning test requires you to identify a word or phrase from a list that means the same or is closest in meaning to a given word or phrase, or has the opposite meaning. Try the following 20 examples (the first has been done for you).

With practice you can greatly improve your performance in this sort of question. If you find these questions difficult then set about expanding your vocabulary and confidence by reading a quality newspaper every day and looking up words whose meaning you do not know in a dictionary or thesaurus. A thesaurus (which lists words of similar meaning) is really helpful in better understanding the answers to these questions.

Q1.

1 Head-on   Hurried
2 Head off
3 Head for
4 Headlong

Answer   ☐

Q1.   Answer Headlong.

Explanation Headlong and hurried are the closest in meaning from the list of options (none is the opposite of hurried).

Q2.

1 Decisive   Deceptive
2 Tortuous
3 Truthful
4 Decision

Answer   ☐

Q3.

1 Salute   Acknowledge
2 Plaudit
3 Obey
4 Slight

Answer   ☐

Q4.

1 Unorthodox   Probable
2 Credible
3 Topic
4 Protect

Answer   ☐

Q5.

1 Relationship   Habitually
2 Lesson
3 Far-reaching
4 Seldom

Answer   ☐

Q6.

1 Glaring   Dazzling
2 Rich
3 Explode
4 Discharge

Answer   ☐

Q7.

1 Nurture   Accomplish
2 Venerate
3 Attain
4 Exclaim

Answer   ☐

Q8.

1 Idea   Thorough
2 Kind
3 Methodical
4 Inconsiderate

Answer   ☐

Q9.

1   Open   Unused
2   Pristine
3   Fake
4   Firsthand

Answer   ☐

Q10.

1   Onlooker   Bystander
2   Security
3   Accomplice
4   Shopper

Answer   ☐

Q11.

1   Comfort   Solemn
2   Informal
3   Blunder
4   Solitary

Answer   ☐

Q12.

1   Fiscal   Economical
2   Generous
3   Business
4   Careful

Answer   ☐

Q13.

1 Launch   Terminate
2 Ultimate
3 Incurable
4 Inherit

Answer [ ]

Q14.

1 Tangible   Untangle
2 Intricate
3 Painstaking
4 Entangle

Answer [ ]

Q15.

1 Harm   Restrain
2 Damp down
3 Cover
4 Dry

Answer [ ]

Q16.

1 Resistant   Incombustible
2 Protectable
3 Flameproof
4 Safe

Answer [ ]

Q17.

1 Speedy   Composure
2 Moderate
3 Panic
4 Attractive

Answer ☐

Q18.

1 Interrupt   Continue
2 Conditional
3 Contention
4 Contentious

Answer ☐

Q19.

1 Exile   Refuge
2 Fugitive
3 Decline
4 Protection

Answer ☐

Q20.

1 Night   Late
2 Hamper
3 Invitation
4 Punctual

Answer ☐

Using numbers

Revise the basics

Practise to become fast, accurate and confident in the key mathematical operations of addition, subtraction, multiplication and simple divisions and percentages. If you are sure that you already are, then feel free to miss this section.

Make sure that you get 100 per cent of these sums right working really quickly. So many tests assume these skills that you must attend on the day able to do them almost without thinking. That will allow you to concentrate on the other components of the questions.

If you need more practice then you will find some very good educational titles that contain lots more practice and explanations than there is room for here. Try titles intended for schools. Alternatively, get someone to help you and make up lots more examples.

There are a number of methods that you can use to answer these questions. Stick to the one you know or that your helper explains to you. For this reason I have not provided explanations to these questions.

Attempt all these questions without using a calculator. See how close you can get to answering the 30 examples in 2 minutes 30 seconds (5 seconds a question!)

Addition

Q1. $5 + 5 =$

Q2. $7 + 8 =$

Q3. $6 + 7 =$

Q4. $7 + 5 =$

Q5. $6 + 8 =$

Q6. $5 + 8 =$

Q7.   3 + 9 =

Q8.   4 + 6 =

Q9.   9 + 4 =

Q10.   2 + 9 =

Q11.   12 + 11 =

Q12.   14 + 13 =

Q13.   15 + 16 =

Q14.   14 + 11 =

Q15.   16 + 17 =

Q16.   15 + 15 =

Q17.   18 + 14 =

Q18.   19 + 17 =

Q19.   13 + 18 =

Q20.   19 + 20 =

Q21. 326 + 363 =

Q22. 542 + 317 =

Q23. 749 + 250 =

Q24. 273 + 361 =

Q25. 824 + 107 =

Q26. 375 + 497 =

Q27. 462 + 498 =

Q28. 800 + 693 =

Q29. 673 + 469 =

Q30. 927 + 784 =

Sums that relate to the calculation of time
Practise to be quick in working with the units hours and minutes; give all answers in hours and minutes.

Q31.   45 minutes + 12 minutes =

Q32.   34 minutes + 1 hour 20 minutes =

Q33.   19 minutes + 25 minutes =

Q34.   17 minutes + 1 hour 38 minutes =

Q35.   09 minutes + 1 hour 11 minutes =

Q36.   1 hour 27 minutes + 19 minutes =

Q37.   15 minutes + 45 minutes =

Q38.   1 hour 16 minutes + 23 minutes =

Q39.   1 hour 04 minutes + 1 hour 52 minutes =

Q40.   1 hour 47 minutes + 56 minutes =

Q41.   39 minutes + 1 hour 47 minutes =

Q42.   1 hour 25 minutes + 1 hour 38 minutes =

Q43.   1 hour 15 minutes + 1 hour 56 minutes =

Q44.   55 minutes + 3 hours 55 minutes =

Q45.   17 minutes + 7 hours 7 minutes =

Q46.   3 hours 59 minutes + 1 hour 29 minutes =

Q47.   5 hours and 17 minutes + 5 hours and 42 minutes =

Q48.   2 hours 15 minutes + 4 hours 45 minutes =

Q49.   4 hours 12 minutes + 7 hours 55 minutes =

Q50.   3 hours 27 minutes + 5 hours 45 minutes =

Subtraction

Attempt all these questions without using a calculator. See how close you can get to answering the 30 examples in 2 minutes 30 seconds (5 seconds a question!)

Q1. $12 - 11 =$

Q2. $14 - 8 =$

Q3. $16 - 9 =$

Q4. $15 - 7 =$

Q5. $23 - 17 =$

Q6. $27 - 19 =$

Q7. $29 - 21 =$

Q8. $31 - 19 =$

Q9. $35 - 26 =$

Q10. $42 - 29 =$

Q11. $324 - 211 =$

Q12. $465 - 305 =$

Q13. $864 - 623 =$

Q14. $999 - 308 =$

Q15. $739 - 526 =$

Q16. $358 - 209 =$

Q17. $421 - 271 =$

Q18. $734 - 198 =$

Q19. $402 - 311 =$

Q20. $605 - 418 =$

Q21.   228 – 179 =

Q22.   452 – 177 =

Q23.   732 – 483 =

Q24.   507 – 312 =

Q25.   921 – 553 =

Q26.   801 – 364 =

Q27.   624 – 289 =

Q28.   500 – 362 =

Q29.   801 – 387 =

Q30.   1000 – 911 =

More sums that relate to the calculation of time

Practise to be quick in working with the units hours and minutes. Do not use a calculator and practise until you are completely familiar with this type of question. Work quickly.

Q1.   45 minutes – 17 minutes =

Q2.   33 minutes – 19 minutes =

Q3.   52 minutes – 45 minutes =

Q4.   31 minutes – 18 minutes =

Q5.   1 hour 12 minutes – 1 hour 06 minutes =

Q6.   1 hour 33 minutes – 20 minutes =

Q7.   1 hour 03 minutes – 15 minutes =

Q8.   1 hour 24 minutes – 33 minutes =

Q9.   1 hour 41 minutes – 1 hour 03 minutes =

Q10.   1 hour 30 minutes – 57 minutes =

Q11.   2 hours 19 minutes – 1 hour 41 minutes =

Q12.   2 hours 36 minutes – 1 hour 14 minutes =

Q13.   2 hours 09 minutes – 1 hour 16 minutes =

Q14.   1 hour 51 minutes – 1 hour 37 minutes =

Q15.   2 hours 24 minutes – 1 hour 29 minutes =

Q16.   2 hours 12 minutes – 1 hour 47 minutes =

Q17.   5 hours 03 minutes – 1 hour 49 minutes =

Q18.   4 hours 18 minutes – 3 hours 53 minutes =

Q19.   5 hours 21 minutes – 1 hour 47 minutes =

Q20.   3 hours 10 minutes – 3 hours 6 minutes =

Q21.   4 hours 18 minutes – 1 hour 07 minutes =

Multiplication

Revise your multiplication tables, if you cannot get these examples right very quickly.

Attempt all these questions without using a calculator. See how close you can get to answering each question in 5 seconds!

Q1. $5 \times 6 =$

Q2. $6 \times 3 =$

Q3. $8 \times 4 =$

Q4. $9 \times 2 =$

Q5. $6 \times 6 =$

Q6. $2 \times 8 =$

Q7. $7 \times 3 =$

Q8. $7 \times 5 =$

Q9. $3 \times 9 =$

Q10. $6 \times 8 =$

Q11. $4 \times 8 =$

Q12. $9 \times 4 =$

Q13. $5 \times 11 =$

Q14. $7 \times 6 =$

Q15. $7 \times 7 =$

Q16. $8 \times 7 =$

Q17. $6 \times 9 =$

Q18. $7 \times 9 =$

Q19. $8 \times 9 =$

Q20. $11 \times 8 =$

Division and percentages

Attempt all these questions without using a calculator. Work as quickly as possible; if you are slow at division then you need to practise your multiplication tables some more. Revise the rules and undertake more practice if there are any questions you cannot do.

Q1. $12 \div 3 =$

Q2. $25 \div 2 =$

Q3. $28 \div 4 =$

Q4. $36 \div 4 =$

Q5. $72 \div 8 =$

Q6. $55 \div 11 =$

Q7. $54 \div 18 =$

Q8. $81 \div 9 =$

Q9. $240 \div 20 =$

Q10. $270 \div 30 =$

Q11.   21% of 100 =

Q12.   30% of 50 =

Q13.   25% of 10 =

Q14.   20% of 75 =

Q15.   7% of 300 =

Q16.   12.5% of 200 =

Q17.   10% of 120 =

Q18.   1% of 250 =

Q19.   60% of 400 =

Q20.   3% of 2,400 =

Using numbers and time

If you face a using numbers or time test, it may well comprise a situation different from the one described here. However, the assumed skills required for this test are likely to be very similar to some real tests, so make sure that you can do this type of question really quickly, getting them right every time without a calculator.

Situation 1

The following situation relates to the 15 questions below:

> Imagine that a firefighter is allocated a response time which starts when an emergency call is received (time of call). The response time varies depending on the location of the incident and the time of day (this is called time allowed). Your task is to calculate the amount of time the firefighter has left in order to complete the task in the response time.

Consider the following example and then practise on the questions that follow:

Q1.

Time of call	11.00
Response time	46 minutes
Time now	11.20
Time left	?

Answer [   ]

Answer 26 minutes.

Explanation The firefighter has 46 minutes in which to respond to the incident beginning from the time of the call. The call was received at 11.00 and the time now is 11.20, so 20 minutes of the response time has passed. This means that the firefighter has 26 minutes left.

Now try these examples:

Q2.

Time of call	08.11
Response time	67 minutes
Time now	08.52
Time left	?

Answer [   ]

Q3.

Time of call	06.53
Response time	41 minutes
Time now	07.28
Time left	?

Answer [   ]

Q4.

Time of call	03.37
Response time	39 minutes
Time now	04.06
Time left	?

Answer [   ]

Q5.

Time of call	04.49
Response time	44 minutes
Time now	05.21
Time left	?

Answer [   ]

Q6.

Time of call	01.39
Response time	49 minutes
Time now	02.18
Time left	?

Answer

Q7.

Time of call	03.03
Response time	99 minutes
Time now	03.47
Time left	?

Answer

Q8.

Time of call	11.51
Response time	48 minutes
Time now	12.15
Time left	?

Answer

Q9.

Time of call	09.41
Response time	40 minutes
Time now	10.13
Time left	?

Answer

Q10.

Time of call	07.04
Response time	98 minutes
Time now	08.41
Time left	?

Answer [   ]

Q11.

Time of call	04.35
Response time	57 minutes
Time now	05.19
Time left	?

Answer [   ]

Q12.

Time of call	03.50
Response time	59 minutes
Time now	04.29
Time left	?

Answer [   ]

Q13.

Time of call	05.52
Response time	71 minutes
Time now	06.44
Time left	?

Answer [   ]

Q14.

Time of call	07.21
Response time	71 minutes
Time now	08.17
Time left	?

Answer [   ]

Q15.

Time of call	08.37
Response time	54 minutes
Time now	09.12
Time left	?

Answer [   ]

More using numbers and time

Situation 2

Imagine a firefighter crew leaving the station to attend an incident. Your task in this situation is to calculate how long the crew have been at the incident. You are given the time that they departed the station (departure time), the time now and the time it took to reach the incident (journey time).

Consider the following example and then try the 14 examples that follow.

Remember a calculator is not allowed. Give all answers in minutes.

Q1.

Departure time	09.00
Time now	10.10
Journey time	15 minutes
Time in attendance	?

Answer [   ]

Answer 55 minutes

Explanation The crew left the station at 09.00 and took 15 minutes to reach the incident. They arrived at the incident therefore at 09.15. The time now is 10.10 so they have so far been at the incident for 55 minutes.

Q2.

Departure time	11.00
Time now	12.20
Journey time	30 minutes
Time in attendance	?

Answer [   ]

Q3.

Departure time   03.20
Time now   05.09
Journey time   16 minutes
Time in attendance   ?

Answer [   ]

Q4.

Departure time   07.50
Time now   08.17
Journey time   9 minutes
Time in attendance   ?

Answer [   ]

Q5.

Departure time   01.40
Time now   02.33
Journey time   21 minutes
Time in attendance   ?

Answer [   ]

Q6.

Departure time   07.31
Time now   09.11
Journey time   36 minutes
Time in attendance   ?

Answer [   ]

Q7.

Departure time   09.10
Time now   11.03
Journey time   45 minutes
Time in attendance ?

Answer   [   ]

Q8.

Departure time   01.56
Time now   02.40
Journey time   29 minutes
Time in attendance ?

Answer   [   ]

Q9.

Departure time   10.07
Time now   11.06
Journey time   31 minutes
Time in attendance ?

Answer   [   ]

Q10.

Departure time   07.18
Time now   08.31
Journey time   7 minutes
Time in attendance ?

Answer   [   ]

Q11.

Departure time   11.01
Time now   12.34
Journey time   49 minutes
Time in attendance   ?

Answer   [   ]

Q12.

Departure time   12.53
Time now   01.40
Journey time   22 minutes
Time in attendance   ?

Answer   [   ]

Q13.

Departure time   08.13
Time now   09.44
Journey time   17 minutes
Time in attendance   ?

Answer   [   ]

Q14.

Departure time   09.54
Time now   10.18
Journey time   23 minutes
Time in attendance   ?

Answer   [   ]

Q15.

Departure time	11.07
Time now	12.45
Journey time	31 minutes
Time in attendance	?

Answer [   ]

Even more using numbers and time

Situation 3

Imagine that you are allocated tasks and a time in which to complete them. This exercise requires that you work out from the information given how much time remains in which you have to complete the task. You are given the following information: time allowed, the time you started and the time now. Try the following 15 examples.

Give all answers in minutes. Remember you are working out the time that remains.

Q1.

Time allowed	60 minutes
Time at start	08.15
Time now	08.31
Time remaining	?

Answer

Q2.

Time allowed	70 minutes
Time at start	08.17
Time now	09.21
Time remaining	?

Answer

Q3.

Time allowed	50 minutes
Time at start	03.40
Time now	04.15
Time remaining	?

Answer

Q4.

Time allowed	100 minutes
Time at start	01.16
Time now	02.31
Time remaining	?

Answer [   ]

Q5.

Time allowed	80 minutes
Time at start	08.27
Time now	09.13
Time remaining	?

Answer [   ]

Q6.

Time allowed	1 hour
Time at start	11.41
Time now	12.19
Time remaining	?

Answer [   ]

Q7.

Time allowed	53 minutes
Time at start	03.37
Time now	04.24
Time remaining	?

Answer [   ]

Q8.

Time allowed	120 minutes
Time at start	05.21
Time now	07.08
Time remaining	?

Answer

Q9.

Time allowed	150 minutes
Time at start	09.18
Time now	10.43
Time remaining	?

Answer

Q10.

Time allowed	46 minutes
Time at start	08.51
Time now	09.17
Time remaining	?

Answer

Q11.

Time allowed	62 minutes
Time at start	03.35
Time now	04.21
Time remaining	?

Answer

Q12.

Time allowed	28 minutes
Time at start	11.45
Time now	12.13
Time remaining	?

Answer

Q13.

Time allowed	1 hour
Time at start	04.51
Time now	05.21
Time remaining	?

Answer

Q14.

Time allowed	180 minutes
Time at start	09.20
Time now	10.53
Time remaining	?

Answer

Q15.

Time allowed	2 hours
Time at start	12.06
Time now	01.57
Time remaining	?

Answer

Numerical reasoning

Sequencing

In this type of question you are given a series of numbers with one or two numbers missing. You have to work out the relationship between the numbers in order to identify correctly the missing numbers from a list of suggested answers. The series of numbers may be presented in a shape, boxes or grid.

Practice will help with this type of question because the questions are largely based on the same type of patterns or rules. Once you realize what to look for you will find you get better and better. Answers and explanations are provided in Chapter 6.

Q1.

18 20 ?? 24 26

A 16
B 21
C 22
D 23

Answer ☐

Q2.

101 103 105 107 ??

A 108
B 109
C 110
D 111

Answer ☐

Q3.

? 14 28 56 112

A 4
B 5
C 6
D 7

Answer   ☐

Q4.

20 23 26 29 ??

A 31
B 32
C 33
D 34

Answer   ☐

Q5.

30 35 ?? 45 50

A 40
B 41
C 42
D 43

Answer   ☐

Q6.

?? 17 10 3

A 25
B 24
C 23
D 22

Answer   ☐

Q7.

36 40 ?? 48

A 42
B 43
C 44
D 45

Answer   ☐

Q8.

72 ?? 38 21

A 40
B 45
C 17
D 55

Answer   ☐

Q9.

5 15 45 ??

A 135
B 75
C 65
D 125

Answer   ☐

Q10.

12 14 26 40 ??

A 52
B 56
C 42
D 66

Answer   ☐

Q11.

40 ?? 56 64

A 46
B 48
C 50
D 64

Answer ☐

Q12.

?? 60 64 68

A 54
B 55
C 56
D 57

Answer ☐

Q13.

132 180 228 ???

A 266
B 276
C 286
D 232

Answer ☐

Q14.

−14 −11 −8 ??

A −3
B −4
C −5
D −6

Answer ☐

Q15.

18 ?? 27 31.5

A 22.5
B 23
C 23.5
D 24

Answer [   ]

Q16.

??? 237.5 225 212.5

A 242.5
B 245
C 247.5
D 250

Answer [   ]

Q17.

6 13 ?? 55

A 27
B 28
C 29
D 30

Answer [   ]

Q18.

54 63 ?? 81

A 70
B 71
C 72
D 73

Answer [   ]

Q19.

250 50 ?? –350

A 150
B –150
C 200
D –200

Answer [   ]

Q20.

5 11 17 ??

A 21
B 22
C 23
D 24

Answer [   ]

Q21.

?? 25 125 625

A –5
B 5
C 10
D 15

Answer [   ]

Q22.

24 33 42 ??

A 48
B 49
C 50
D 51

Answer [   ]

Q23.

21 31.5 ?? 52.5

A 42
B 42.5
C 53
D 43.5

Answer   ☐

Q24.

−2 ?? −36 −53

A −17
B −18
C −19
D −20

Answer   ☐

Q25.

297 ?? 33 11

A 96
B 97
C 98
D 99

Answer   ☐

Q26.

−20 −3 ?? 31

A 12
B 13
C 14
D 15

Answer   ☐

Q27.

? 14 41 122

A 5
B 6
C 7
D 8

Answer ⬚

Q28.

?? 56 63 70

A 48
B 49
C 50
D 51

Answer ⬚

Q29.

5 7.5 12.5 ??

A 18.5
B 19
C 19.5
D 20

Answer ⬚

Q30.

??? 156 168 180

A 144
B 145
C 146
D 180

Answer ⬚

Non-verbal reasoning

These questions involve the identification of relationships between shapes. Some Fire Authorities still use this sort of question but it is likely to become less common and is unlikely to feature in the new tests under the national standards.

Below are 40 examples, 20 each of two styles of question. Practise at these styles of question will allow you to become familiar with the typical demands of these questions. With this sort of practice you will find that you can answer this type of question more quickly and with greater confidence.

Answers and explanations are provided on pages 210–215.

Question type 1

Identify the quality that is common to the two question shapes and then decide which of the question shapes A, B or C shares this quality.

Q1.

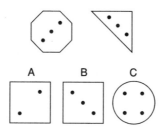

Answer   ☐

Q2.

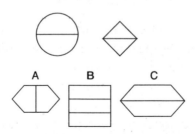

Answer ☐

Q3.

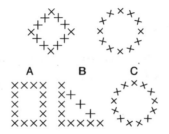

Answer ☐

Q4.

● ○ ○ ● ●   ● ● ○ ○ ●

A   B   C
○ ● ● ● ○   ● ● ● ○ ○   ● ○ ● ○ ●

Answer ☐

Q5.

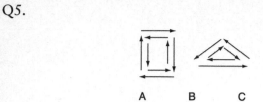

Answer ☐

Q6.

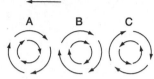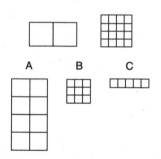

Answer ☐

Q7.

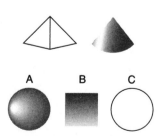

Answer ☐

Q8.

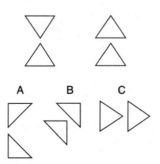

Answer ☐

Q9.

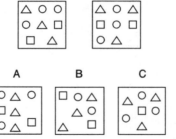

Answer ☐

Q10.

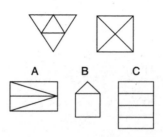

Answer ☐

Q11.

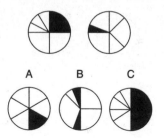

Answer [ ]

Q12.

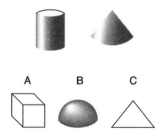

Answer [ ]

Q13.

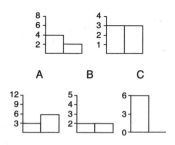

Answer [ ]

Q14.

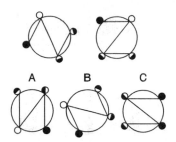

Answer ☐

Q15.

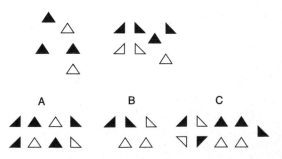

Answer ☐

Q16.

Answer ☐

Q17.

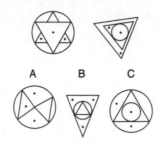

Answer ☐

Q18.

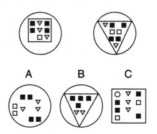

Answer ☐

Q19.

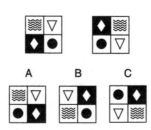

Answer ☐

Q20.

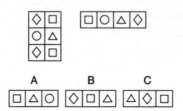

Answer ☐

Question type 2

Complete the sequence by identifying which of the question shapes should be placed in this empty space. Note that some of the diagrams are numbered to indicate in which direction the sequence runs. As in most tests, the questions start easy and get harder.

Q21.

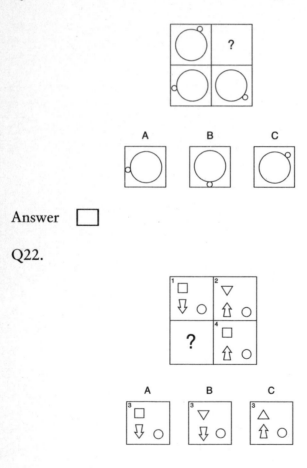

Answer ☐

Q22.

Answer ☐

Q23.

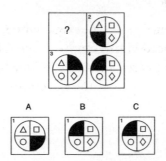

A   B   C

Answer ☐

Q24.

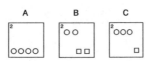

A   B   C

Answer ☐

Q25.

A   B   C

Answer ☐

Q26.

A   B   C

Answer ☐

Q27.

A   B   C

Answer ☐

Q28.

A   B   C

Answer ☐

Q29.

Answer ☐

Q30.

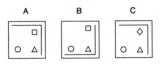

Answer ☐

Q31.

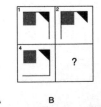

Answer ☐

Q32.

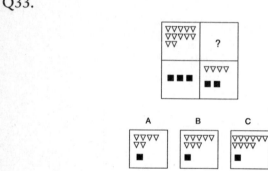

Answer [ ]

Q33.

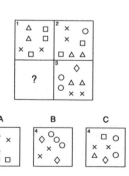

Answer [ ]

Q34.

Answer [ ]

Q35.

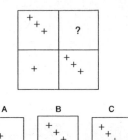

Answer ☐

Q36.

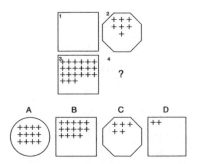

Answer ☐

Q37.

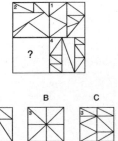

Answer ☐

Q38.

Answer ☐

Q39.

Answer ☐

Q40.

Answer ☐

Tests of observation

Some authorities are using a test of observation. These tests involve watching a short video and then, once it has finished, answering a series of questions about it. It is possible that you have to watch a series of short video clips and answer questions after each short clip.

It helps if you can take notes during the video. The briefing before the video begins may well give an indication of what to look out for. Some of the videos lend themselves to you drawing a map and making notes at the points at which you see particular items. It is important that you are able to make notes while still watching, otherwise you risk missing important detail while writing or drawing.

A useful tip is to devise beforehand suitable abbreviations. Using these can save you a lot of time when note taking. They can also help avoid the problem that you cannot remember what your note stood for once you start answering the questions. For example, if you see two brown bags it is far quicker to write 2bb but you need to take care that you remember that bb stood for brown bag as it could also mean black box or blue bin. So decide in advance on convenient, unique abbreviations and stick to them while note taking.

Practice tests

This chapter comprises 5 realistic practice tests. Use them to develop a winning test strategy under the pressure of time.

To get the most from these practice tests you should try to create as realistic a test situation as possible. Work in a quiet place without interruption and be strict about stopping when you have used up all the time allowed. Use the last few minutes to attempt all remaining questions.

If you run out of time before you have attempted all the questions then you need to increase the speed at which you work and not fall into the trap of spending too long on any one question.

Realize that to do well in a test you really have to try hard and you should, when the test is finished, feel exhausted from the exertion. If you do not, then you have probably not applied yourself sufficiently.

If you hit a string of questions to which you do not know the answer then keep going as you may find the next line of questions far more approachable.

Make sure that you pay attention to how many questions you have attempted. In some of the tests, at the bottom of each page you are told to turn over the page. This means that there are more questions to go.

Answers and many explanations are found on pages 215–231.

Practice test 1

Read each passage and answer the questions that follow. There are 6 passages each followed by 5 questions.

You have 12 minutes in which to attempt all 30 questions.

Only refer to information provided in the passage to answer the questions. Work quickly and indicate whether you consider the statement to be true, false or that you cannot tell.

Please note that the content of the passages is intended only to provide realistic test practice. They do not necessarily report accurately what you should do if a fire occurs or accurately report the responsibilities of employers or the Fire Authorities.

Should you wish to obtain such advice then contact your local fire station or visit sites such as www.firekills-gov.uk/.

Do not turn the page until you are told to begin.

Passage 1

We can all recognize fire but the majority of us fail to fully understand it. Once started, fire may grow unexpectedly fast and in very little time it can threaten life and property. The potential for an accidental fire exists in a large number of everyday activities, including driving a car, cooking, using electrical equipment and going about our daily work.

Every year people are killed, and even more are injured, by fires that occur in the workplace, whilst travelling and in the home. The cost of a fire in terms of the loss of possessions and as an interruption to business can be equally devastating. The cost to business through fire runs to many millions of pounds every year and some companies fail to recover from its effects.

Q1.　If a fire occurs a business is unlikely to recover from it.

　　　True
　　　False
　　　Cannot say

　　　Answer [   ]

Q2.　Fires once they start can grow at an alarming rate.

　　　True
　　　False
　　　Cannot say

　　　Answer [   ]

Turn over the page.

Q3.   When driving a car there is always a risk of an accidental fire occurring.

True
False
Cannot say

Answer [   ]

Q4.   While most people do not fully understand fire, fire-fighters because of their training do.

True
False
Cannot say

Answer [   ]

Q5.   More people die in accidental fires at work, home and while travelling than are injured by them.

True
False
Cannot say

Answer [   ]

Turn over the page.

Passage 2

Every business should ensure that employees know what to do in the event of a fire. Time must also be taken to ensure that staff know how to prevent accidental fires in the first place. These simple precautions could save a business from having to face the devastating effects of an accidental fire and for this reason alone taking such precautions makes sound business sense. However, the law also compels most employers to provide adequate training in fire awareness and fire safety for all members of their staff.

The United Kingdom's Fire Authorities are recognized throughout the world as a leading voice in fire safety. They have earned this recognition because of the many decades of experience they have and because their workforce is trained to the very highest standards.

Q6. Complying with the law is not the only reason why an employer should ensure that staff know what to do in the event of a fire.

True
False
Cannot say

Answer [   ]

Q7. An accidental fire can have a devastating effect on a business.

True
False
Cannot say

Answer [   ]

Turn over the page.

Q8.   All employers are compelled by law to provide adequate training in fire awareness.

True
False
Cannot say

Answer [   ]

Q9.   The UK's fire authorities have staff trained to a very high standard.

True
False
Cannot say

Answer [   ]

Q10.   An employer can be prosecuted if they fail to provide fire safety training to their staff.

True
False
Cannot say

Answer [   ]

Turn over the page.

Passage 3

So many fires in the home start at night when the occupants are asleep that everyone should have a fire safety routine before they go to bed. Such a routine involves switching off and unplugging any electrical appliance that is not designed to stay on. So switch off and unplug everything other than, for example, the video and fridge. If anyone smokes in the house, make sure that any cigarettes are extinguished and that the contents of ashtrays are cold. Discourage anyone in the household from smoking in bed. If you have an open fire, let it burn well down before you go to bed and always use a spark guard. Do not be tempted to run a washing machine at night as these can catch fire when operating and are not designed to be on all the time. Close all doors throughout your property as this will slow down the spread of any heat or smoke generated by a fire. Practise such a routine every evening and your home will be considerably safer from the threat of a fire.

Q11. More accidental fires start at night than during the day.

   True
   False
   Cannot say

   Answer [   ]

Q12. You should unplug the washing machine at night.

   True
   False
   Cannot say

   Answer [   ]

Turn over the page.

Q13. Open fires should have a guard in front of them in order to stop sparks.

True
False
Cannot say

Answer

Q14. The advice to have a fire safety routine does not apply to people who live alone.

True
False
Cannot say

Answer

Q15. Heat and smoke generated by a fire can spread through a house; closing doors helps slow down this effect.

True
False
Cannot say

Answer

Turn over the page.

Passage 4

Fit a smoke alarm in your home and it could save your life. If you already have a smoke alarm then make sure that it is operational by testing it. Regularly check that the battery is not flat otherwise it will fail to warn you should a fire occur.

You can buy smoke alarms for under £5 from a DIY, electrical or hardware shop. Some garages and supermarkets also sell them. Fit a smoke alarm between your living area and the bedrooms. Ideally, you should fit one in every room except the bedrooms. Make sure that you can hear it throughout your home, especially in the bedrooms. Test it each month by pressing the test button. Change the battery every year. From time to time, use a vacuum cleaner to get rid of any dust inside.

If the low battery warning sounds (usually an intermittent bleep), replace the battery with a new one. If you have difficulty in hearing then you can buy a smoke alarm that has a vibrating pad or flashing light. Further information on these products can be obtained from the Royal National Institute for the Deaf or from your local fire station. Remember that a smoke alarm is useless if it does not have a battery or if the battery is flat.

Q16. Smoke alarms are cheapest in supermarkets.

    True
    False
    Cannot say

    Answer

Q17. Ideally you should fit a smoke alarm in every room especially in the bedrooms.

True
False
Cannot say

Answer [   ]

Turn over the page.

Q18. The passage states that you should test a smoke alarm every month and vacuum it to remove dust once a year.

True
False
Cannot say

Answer [   ]

Q19. Special smoke alarms are available for people with a disability.

True
False
Cannot say

Answer [   ]

Q20. The passage provides advice that, if followed, could save lives.

True
False
Cannot say

Answer [   ]

Turn over the page.

Passage 5

Most employers are required by law under the Fire Precautions Workplace Regulations 1997 to carry out a fire risk assessment and record the findings of that assessment. They must also provide and maintain precautions to keep people safe from fire in the workplace and provide information, instructions and training to staff about fire precautions. They must also provide a written fire emergency plan.

Local Fire Authorities are responsible for the supervision and enforcement of the regulations. A Fire Safety Inspecting Officer can inhibit the use of a part or all of a building from immediate effect if she or he thinks it is unsafe. They can also issue an enforcement notice requiring improvements to be made. Failure of an employer to comply with the regulations is a criminal act and the Fire Authorities may prosecute in the courts.

Q21. Employers must record the conclusions of their fire risk assessment.

True
False
Cannot say

Answer

Q22. Employers must have a written fire emergency plan.

True
False
Cannot say

Answer

Turn over the page.

Q23. A Fire Safety Inspecting Officer can stop people from working in a part of a building if they consider it unsafe.

True
False
Cannot say

Answer

Q24. Fire Authorities have the power to prosecute; however, this would be the last resort.

True
False
Cannot say

Answer

Q25. The passage states that local fire authorities are responsible for keeping people safe from fire at work.

True
False
Cannot say

Answer

Turn over the page.

Passage 6

As well as complying with the fire regulations, some premises also require a fire certificate. These are legal documents that set out the fire precautionary arrangements of the building. Fire certificates are required if the premises are hotels or boarding houses which provide sleeping accommodation for six or more people or if sleeping accommodation is provided above the first floor or below ground level. Factories, shops, offices and railway stations at which more than 20 people work at any one time must also obtain certificates. Any site at which explosive or highly flammable material is stored must also obtain a fire certificate.

Q26. A three-storey hotel with accommodation for five people requires a fire certificate.

True
False
Cannot say

Answer [   ]

Q27. A railway station at which 20 people worked would require a fire certificate.

True
False
Cannot say

Answer [   ]

Turn over the page.

Q28. A firework warehouse which employs only a night watchman requires a fire certificate.

True
False
Cannot say

Answer [   ]

Q29. A large shop in which 30 people work but not all at the same time requires a fire certificate.

True
False
Cannot say

Answer [   ]

Q30. If an employer has a fire certificate for their premises then they do not have to comply with the fire regulations.

True
False
Cannot say

Answer [   ]

End of test.

Practice test 2

Using numbers and time

25-question quick test

This test comprises 25 questions which test your command of the key skills examined by real firefighter tests.

Allow yourself 13 minutes in which to complete the test. Really go for it and do not stop until you run out of time.

You will need to work as quickly as possible.

Do not use a calculator.

Do not turn the page until you are ready to begin.

Q1. The time now is 12.16. What was the time 55 minutes ago?

Answer

Q2. The time now is 03.40. What was the time 2 hours and 16 minutes ago?

Answer

Q3. The time now is 04.07. What was the time 33 minutes ago?

Answer

Q4. The time now is 12.03. What was the time 1 hour 47 minutes ago?

Answer

Q5. If the time now is 06.21, what was the time 51 minutes ago?

Answer

Q6. An emergency call was logged at 21.00 hours and the time now is 22.17. How many minutes have passed since the emergency call was logged?

Answer

Q7. If a block of flats contains 24 dwellings, 4 on each floor, how many storeys high is the block?

Answer

Q8. Your colleagues responded to an emergency 50 minutes ago. The time now is 04.23. What was the time when the response began?

Answer

Q9.   If one in three households does not have a working smoke alarm, how many homes are unprotected in a town of 2,100 homes?

Answer

Q10. If you entered a smoke filled house at 09.41 and the time is now 10.13, how long have you been in the building?

Answer

Q11. 320 people were present in a building when the practice evacuation took place. The fire marshal reported 281 people assembled at the meeting place. How many people were unaccounted for?

Answer

Q12. If a burning vehicle is reported at 12.44 and the emergency services arrive at the scene at 13.12, how long was the interval between the report and the arrival of the emergency services?

Answer

Q13. One in five calls to the emergency services are hoax calls; if a fire station receives 30 calls a week, how many are likely to be hoaxes?

Answer

Q14. If the time now is 13.52, what will be the time in 37 minutes?

Answer

Q15. If a block of flats comprises nine floors, each with three flats, how many flats are there in the block?

Answer

Q16. If an emergency call was made at 01.13 and it took 25 minutes for the fire crew to reach the location of the emergency, what was the time when the fire crew arrived at the scene?

Answer

Q17. If two in five households include at least one person who smokes, how many homes from a total of 200 includes one smoker or more?

Answer

Q18. Three hours and 20 minutes is how many minutes?

Answer

Q19. In an incident 13 people were reported missing while 297 were accounted for. What is the total count of people involved?

Answer

Q20. An emergency call was logged at 09.21 and the time now is 10.07. How many minutes have passed since the emergency call was logged?

Answer

Q21. One in four calls to the emergency service are fire related. If a total of 280 calls are received, how many would you expect to be fire related?

Answer

Q22. Your colleagues responded to an emergency 70 minutes ago, and the time now is 01.15. What was the time when the response began?

Answer

Q23. To stay fit a firefighter went on a 2 km run, 3 times a week. How many kilometres did she run in a six-week period?

Answer [   ]

Q24. If you entered a smoke-filled room at 03.11 and the time is now 04.03, how long have you been in the building?

Answer [   ]

Q25. In a 50-hour period of duty a watch was out responding to emergencies 12 per cent of the time. For how much time was the watch not out responding to emergencies?

Answer [   ]

End of test.

Practice test 3

Verbal reasoning

This test comprises 30 questions. The first 14 are a type of verbal reasoning question. The style of question then changes to another kind of verbal reasoning question for the remaining 16.

The first 14 questions require you to identify, from a list, a missing word or phrase from two pairs of words. To find the correct word or phrase you have to study the complete pair and identify the relationship that exists between the items that make up the pair. You then must choose a word or phrase from the list that completes the second pair and maintains the same relationship.

Your task in type 2 questions is to identify, from a list, a word or phrase that means the same or has the closest meaning to or means the opposite of the word or phrase on the left.

If you are sufficiently practised in verbal reasoning questions then you will have no difficulty in switching between the styles of question. If you find that you have to go back and reread the instructions before you can complete the second style of question then you should undertake more practice in verbal reasoning.

Answers and some explanations are provided on pages 221–223. Once you have finished the test, check your answers, making sure that you look up the meaning of any words that you did not understand and the words of questions that you got wrong.

You are allowed 20 minutes in which to complete the test. Work quickly and without interruption and write the number of the word of your choice from the list in the answer box.

If you find a series of questions difficult then keep going; you may find that you reach questions later on for which you are better prepared. Remember that to do well in a test you have to try really hard.

Do not turn over the page until you are ready to begin.

Type 1
Q1.

Tabloid	Broadsheet
?	Spanish

1 European
2 Hindi
3 Mediterranean
4 American

Answer [   ]

Q2.

?	Surf
Candle	Light

1 Wash powder
2 Sport
3 Ripple
4 Wave

Answer [   ]

Q3.

Graphite	?
Furniture	Wood

1 Pencil
2 Slippery
3 Organic
4 Carbon

Answer [   ]

Q4.

Medicine   Cure
?   Warmth
1 Summer
2 Insulation
3 Hospitality
4 Fire

Answer [   ]

Q5.

House   Bricks
Pension   ?
1 Financial institution
2 Savings
3 Retirement
4 Contributions

Answer [   ]

Q6.

Inference   ?
Seed   Plant
1 Premise
2 Slander
3 Conclusion
4 Reaction

Answer [   ]

Q7.

Cruel   ?
Harmony   Discord
1 Inhumane
2 Sadistic
3 Criminal
4 Humane

Answer [   ]

Q8.

Air   Breathe
?   Solution
1 Problem
2 Answer
3 Liquid
4 Compound

Answer [   ]

Q9.

?   Ascend
Pledge   Guarantee
1 Block
2 Scale
3 Descend
4 Retract

Answer [   ]

Q10.

Pencil	Art
?	Telecommunications

1 Phone
2 Communication
3 Watch dog
4 Artist

Answer

Q11.

Sun	?
Criticism	Anger

1 Day
2 Tan
3 Burn
4 Light

Answer

Q12.

Know	No
?	Site

1 Sight
2 Location
3 Situation
4 Building

Answer

Q13.

Music	Pleasure
?	Discovery

1 Loss
2 Research
3 Find
4 Adventure

Answer [   ]

Q14.

Outspoken	Reserved
General	?

1 Specific
2 Generic
3 Officer
4 Widespread

Answer [   ]

Type 2
Q15.

Prevention   ?
                  1 Cure
                  2 Elimination
                  3 Evasion
                  4 Safety

Answer [   ]

Q16.

Investigate   ?
                  1 Detective
                  2 Ignorant
                  3 Ignore
                  4 Inquest

Answer [   ]

Q17.

Assessment   ?
                      1 Evaluation
                      2 Incident
                      3 Strong point
                      4 Situation

Answer   [   ]

Q18.

Escape   ?
                      1 Lucky
                      2 Route
                      3 Remain
                      4 Plan

Answer   [   ]

Q19.

Regulations   ?
                      1 Safety
                      2 Chaos
                      3 Anarchy
                      4 Code

Answer   [   ]

Q20.

Affirmative   ?
                      1 Swear
                      2 Comfort
                      3 Declare
                      4 Negative

Answer   [   ]

Q21.

Support   ?
                   1 Install
                   2 Brace
                   3 Go backwards
                   4 Return

Answer   [   ]

Q22.

Ignore   ?
                   1 Insult
                   2 Forget
                   3 Consult
                   4 Lose

Answer   [   ]

Q23.

?   Utilize
                   1 Organize
                   2 Use up
                   3 Knife and fork
                   4 Deploy

Answer   [   ]

Q24.

Neighbourly   ?
                   1 Sociable
                   2 Collective
                   3 Public
                   4 Team player

Answer   [   ]

Q25.

?   Drought
                  1 Drunk
                  2 Deluge
                  3 Drown
                  4 Famine

Answer

Q26.

?   Enslave
                  1 Criminal
                  2 Colonial
                  3 Liberate
                  4 Genocide

Answer

Q27.

Forthright   ?
                  1 Debate
                  2 Conceal
                  3 Forth place
                  4 Wrong

Answer

Q28.

Affliction   ?
                  1 Console
                  2 Make worse
                  3 Persecute
                  4 Ordeal

Answer

Q29.

?   Collapse
                     1 Overthrow
                     2 Disintegrate
                     3 Defend
                     4 Enflame

Answer [   ]

Q30.

Extinguish   ?
                   1 Quench
                   2 Squeeze
                   3 Prevent
                   4 Famous

Answer [   ]

End of test.

Practice test 4

Sequencing

This test comprises two styles of question.

In the first type you are presented with a series of numbers presented in a row of boxes; one number is missing. You are offered a choice of four suggested answers and it is your task to identify the suggested answer that correctly completes the sequence. You record the number of the suggested answer in the answer box.

The second style of question comprises a square divided into nine boxes with a number in each box except two. It is your task to identify the missing numbers from a list of four pairs. The answers are found by identifying a constant relationship that applies across the boxes (the rows) and another relationship that applies down the boxes (the columns).

If you are sufficiently practised in numerical reasoning questions then you will have no difficulty in switching between these styles of questions. If you find the switch difficult, for example if you find that you have to go back and reread the instructions before you can proceed, then you should undertake more practice of numerical reasoning questions before taking a real test.

Answers and explanations are provided on pages 224–226. Once you have finished the test, check your answers, making sure that if you got any wrong you work to understand where you went wrong.

This test comprises 30 questions. You are allowed 20 minutes in which to complete the test. Work quickly and without interruption.

Do not use a calculator.

Do not turn over the page until you are ready to begin.

Q1.

| 16 | ? | 64 | 128 |

1 20
2 32
3 40
4 46

Answer

Q2.

| 27 | 36 | ? | 54 |

1 43
2 44
3 45
4 46

Answer

Q3.

| 20 | 30 | ? | 90 | 170 |

1 50
2 40
3 30
4 20

Answer

Q4.

| 33 | 27 | 21 | ? |

1 16
2 17
3 14
4 15

Answer

Q5.

90	?	64	51

1 76
2 77
3 78
4 79

Answer

Q6.

?	6	9
6	?	18
12	24	36

1 2, 4
2 9, 9
3 3, 12
4 3, 9

Answer

Q7.

12	24	48
18	36	72
24	?	?

1 48, 84
2 42, 96
3 42, 84
4 48, 96

Answer

Q8.

?	100	200
25	?	100
12.5	25	50

1 25, 50
2 50, 50
3 50, 75
4 50, 25

Answer

Q9.

4	8	12
12	24	?
?	72	108

1 36, 36
2 24, 48
3 18, 36
4 48, 48

Answer

Q10.

15	30	?
30	60	90
60	?	180

1 50, 100
2 60, 120
3 45, 120
4 60, 90

Answer

Q11.

?	19	29
18	38	58
36	76	?

1 10, 98
2 6, 96
3 9, 106
4 9, 116

Answer [   ]

Q12.

20	40	?
15	?	60
10	20	40

1 60, 45
2 80, 30
3 45, 50
4 50, 30

Answer [   ]

Q13.

10	5	?
20	10	?
40	20	10

1 10, 20
2 2.5, 5
3 0, 0
4 7.5, 2.5

Answer [   ]

Q14.

12	?	30
24	42	?
48	84	120

1   21, 60
2   15, 56
3   20, 50
4   23, 48

Answer

Q15.

40	30	20
?	15	10
10	?	5

1   30, 8
2   25, 7
3   20, 6
4   20, 7.5

Answer

Q16.

17	?	5
51	33	15
153	99	?

1   14, 33
2   13, 30
3   11, 45
4   9, 45

Answer

Q17.

8	?	72
13	39	117
18	?	162

1 24, 54
2 16, 36
3 16, 54
4 24, 36

Answer

Q18.

?	12	4
27	9	3
?	6	2

1 24, 12
2 33, 13
3 18, 12
4 36, 18

Answer

Q19.

42	28	14
21	14	7
?	7	?

1 7.5, 7.5
2 10.5, 3.5
3 10, 4
4 11, 3

Answer

Q20.

21	42	84
14	?	56
7	?	28

1   21, 35
2   28, 14
3   28, 18
4   22, 9

Answer

Q21.

54	27	?
48	24	12
42	21	?

1   13.5, 10.5
2   21.5, 7
3   9, 7
4   9, 10.5

Answer

Q22.

156	168	170	?

1   180
2   181
3   182
4   183

Answer

Q23.

50.0	?	81.0	96.5

1 65.5
2 66.5
3 67.0
4 68.0

Answer

Q24.

8	?	26	50	98

1 12
2 13
3 14
4 15

Answer

Q25.

100	50	–50	?	–50

1 0
2 –25
3 25
4 75

Answer

Q26.

56	70	84	?

1 96
2 97
3 98
4 99

Answer

Q27.

10	15	25	?

1 30
2 40
3 50
4 60

Answer

Q28.

4.0	10.0	25.0	?

1 45.5
2 45.0
3 50.0
4 62.5

Answer

Q29.

?	1.0	4.0	16.0

1 0.33
2 –1.0
3 0.5
4 0.25

Answer

Q30.

64	80	?	112

1 96
2 97
3 98
4 99

Answer

Practice test 5

Learning information

Instructions

If in your real exam to become a firefighter you face a test that requires you to listen to an audio passage and then answer questions, these practice questions will give you a real sense of what to expect and allow you to develop a winning approach.

To benefit from this practice, however, you will need someone's help. You will need to get someone to read the passages to you and then you can answer the questions.

Do not read the passages yourself because if you do you are not practising listening and remembering things and this is the skill examined in this test.

You do not need to set a time limit because the longer you take the harder it gets to remember what you heard. Try taking notes but be careful that you do not miss the next bit of information while you write. Some people find it useful to leave any question that they cannot immediately answer to last.

Each passage is on a separate page and the questions are over the page.

Do not turn over the page until you are ready to begin the practice and remember that to get the most out of this practice you should not read the passages yourself.

Note to the passage reader

Read each passage only once at a slow and steady rate. Advise when you are to start and when the passage is finished. Then instruct the test taker to turn over the page and begin the questions. Do not allow them to read the passage, nor should they see the questions until after they have heard the passage. If they wish they may take notes on a separate piece of paper.

Passage 1

Youngsters setting fire to rubbish and misusing fireworks in the Southfield area of Newbury are endangering their own and others' lives. A fire appliance and crew will visit the area on Sunday and the firefighters will try to talk to the young people about fire safety.

The police will be visiting local traders to discourage them from selling fireworks to anyone under the age of 18 and they will be arresting anyone, and visiting the parents of young offenders, found to be throwing fireworks or lighting fires or engaging in any other sort of dangerous behaviour.

Officers and firefighters are very concerned that someone could end up hurt. Every year over 543 people in the age range 16 to 18 are seriously injured by fireworks.

Q1.   Southfield is in Newport.

True
False
Cannot say

Answer [   ]

Q2.   The fire appliance is due to visit the area on Saturday.

True
False
Cannot say

Answer [   ]

Q3.   Over 500 people a year aged 16 to 18 are injured by fire-
       works.

True
False
Cannot say

Answer [   ]

Q4.   Local traders have been selling fireworks to the young-
       sters.

True
False
Cannot say

Answer [   ]

Turn over the page.

Q5. Someone has already been hurt by the youngsters' behaviour.

True
False
Cannot say

Answer [   ]

Do not turn over the page until you have heard the next passage.

Passage 2

The fire service not only puts out fires but also works to ensure that they do not happen in the first place. Where there is the greatest risk of fires the service will make the greatest effort to reduce that risk. The principal way in which the fire service will try to prevent fires is through raising awareness and under-standing of fire safety issues. Greatest efforts will be made to educate members of the public most likely to be a victim of fire, for example the elderly, those living alone and smokers.

Community fire-safety schemes will operate from fire stations and firefighters will spend time in the community advising, for example, employers on their fire-safety precau-tions and installing smoke alarms in the homes of members of the public who are at most risk of fire. Already over 13,000 smoke alarms, with batteries that last 10 years, have been fitted under this initiative. Fire stations will be open to the public offering advice on fire and community safety. Wherever possible they will be made fully accessible to people with disabilities.

Q6.   You can get a free smoke alarm from your local fire safety scheme.

   True
   False
   Cannot say

   Answer [   ]

Q7.   All fire stations will be open to the public.

   True
   False
   Cannot say

   Answer [   ]

Q8.   The batteries in the smoke alarms have to be changed every year.

   True
   False
   Cannot say

   Answer [   ]

Q9.   All fire stations will be made accessible to people with disabilities.

   True
   False
   Cannot say

   Answer [   ]

Turn over the page.

Q10. 13,000 smoke alarms have already been fitted by the fire
       service.

       True
       False
       Cannot say

       Answer [   ]

Do not turn over the page until you have heard the next
passage.

Passage 3

Over a five-year period 418 people died in fires in London and an analysis of those tragic deaths found that those at most risk of dying in a fire in their home were people over 60 years of age, who live alone and who smoke and drink and do not have an operational smoke alarm. It was also found that people were more at risk if they lived in three of the London Boroughs.

Over half of the accidental fire deaths in the home were caused by smoking or matches; cooking was the next most common cause, giving rise to almost 20 per cent of the deaths, followed by candles which caused a further 10 per cent of the tragedies.

Alcohol was found to have played a role in a third of the fatal accidents and men were more likely than women to be a victim of such an accident. It was also found that a higher proportion of deaths occurred in winter.

Q11. Smoking or matches caused over half of the accidental fire deaths in the home.

True
False
Cannot say

Answer [   ]

Q12. Residents of four London boroughs have a higher risk of dying in an accidental home fire.

True
False
Cannot say

Answer [   ]

Q13. In the winter months men are more likely to die in an accidental fire in the home.

True
False
Cannot say

Answer [   ]

Q14. Cooking causes 20 per cent of deaths from accidental home fires.

True
False
Cannot say

Answer [   ]

Turn over the page.

Q15. People who smoke and drink alcohol, who are aged over
60 and live alone are most at risk.

True
False
Cannot say

Answer

Do not turn over the page until you have heard the next
passage.

Passage 4

Yorkshire firefighters taking part in the national extraction competition were awarded second place. The competition involves teams of firefighters from all over the country demonstrating their skills at cutting out and removing casualties from serious road traffic accidents.

The competitions are held every two years and teams are judged as they cut trapped dummies from a simulated two-car accident. They are allowed 20 minutes and must work with hydraulic tools and power-driven saws to extract the victims safely.

First place was awarded to a team from South Wales and in total 30 teams took part.

It is believed that the competitions greatly improve the teams' skills in this challenging part of a firefighter's job and are invaluable in the real-life situations they face.

Q16. The competition is held annually.

True
False
Cannot say

Answer [   ]

Q17. The Yorkshire team came second.

True
False
Cannot say

Answer [   ]

Q18. The simulated accident involves two dummies.

True
False
Cannot say

Answer [   ]

Q19. The teams have 20 minutes in which to free the dummies.

True
False
Cannot say

Answer [   ]

Turn over the page.

Q20. The passage suggests that the competition is international.

True
False
Cannot say

Answer [   ]

Do not turn over the page until you have heard the next passage.

Passage 5

The most common sort of fire in the kitchen is caused by deep fat frying. It is an accident that is shockingly common and 4,000 people are injured each year in the UK by this sort of fire.

These fires could all be avoided if people practised some basic rules when doing this sort of cooking. First of all, people must realize that they are doing something really quite dangerous – they are heating on average a litre of oil to a high temperature. This oil can cause serious burns if spilt and it can also catch fire. Once alight it is difficult to put out.

The safest way to deep fry is to use an electric deep fryer that has a fitted thermostat control which prevents the oil from overheating. If such a fryer is unavailable the risk of an accident can be reduced if people:

- do not fill the pan more than one-third full of oil;
- never leave the kitchen when they are deep fat frying;
- turn the heat off if the oil begins to smoke and allow it to cool;
- fry only food that has been dried before it is put in the oil (water on the food could cause the oil to explode).

Q21. Deep fat frying is dangerous.

True
False
Cannot say

Answer [   ]

Q22. The most common sort of fire is caused by deep fat frying.

True
False
Cannot say

Answer [   ]

Q23. Water can cause the oil to explode.

True
False
Cannot say

Answer [   ]

Q24. The average quantity of oil used in a deep fat fryer is one litre.

True
False
Cannot say

Answer [   ]

Turn over the page.

Q25. A pan should not be more than 33.3 per cent full.

True
False
Cannot say

Answer [   ]

Do not turn over the page until you have heard the next passage.

Passage 6

A simulated chemical attack on the London Underground took place over the bank holiday so that the emergency services could practise dealing with a major incident of this kind. In the simulation casualties had to wait half an hour for help to arrive. It took three hours before the last casualty was brought to street level.

The Commissioner of the Fire Brigade concluded that the emergency services would have to find ways in which they could more quickly reach victims of any future real attack. He felt this was bound to be one of the major lessons learnt from the exercise at Bank Station.

The exercise took place under the financial centre of the capital city and was intended to be as realistic as possible. The emergency service staff wore full gas protection suits during the exercise and filled dummies were used as victims, each of which weighed 13 stones. However, the firefighters were not allowed to carry the dummies to the surface as the Health and Safety Executive felt that their weight represented too great a risk to the firefighters' health. The dummies were dragged to the surface instead.

Q26. It took over three hours before the last victim was brought to ground level.

True
False
Cannot say

Answer

Q27. The dummies weighed 13 stones.

True
False
Cannot say

Answer

Q28. The exercise was held in Euston Station.

True
False
Cannot say

Answer

Q29. It must have been hot working in the gas protection suits.

True
False
Cannot say

Answer

Turn over the page.

Q30. It is fair to say that it took the emergency services longer than they expected to get to the victims.

True
False
Cannot say

Answer [   ]

Do not turn over the page until you have heard the next passage.

Passage 7

The White Paper 'Our Fire and Rescue Service' sets out the government's strategy for achieving a modern fire and rescue service in England and Wales.

The report argues that the service must develop a broader role in the prevention of fires and be able to respond to a wider range of threats and hazards, thereby creating safer communities for us all.

The priorities of the service are stated as: working to prevent fires and, when they occur, to save lives and reduce injuries, and to plan for emergencies and environmental disasters and the growing threat of terrorism.

Q31. The government's strategy is intended for the whole of Great Britain.

True
False
Cannot say

Answer

Q32. The role of the service has been widened.

True
False
Cannot say

Answer

Q33. The government's report was described in the passage as a Green Paper.

True
False
Cannot say

Answer

Q34. The growing threat of terrorism is one reason behind the changes posed in the passage.

True
False
Cannot say

Answer

Turn over the page.

Q35. The passage states the priorities of the fire and rescue
service.

True
False
Cannot say

Answer [   ]

Do not turn over the page until you have heard the next
passage.

Passage 8

The largest single cause of deaths and injuries from fire is accidental fires in the home. There is a growing trend in deliberate fires, up by 25 per cent since 1996. Those most likely to be at risk from fire, whether accidental or deliberately set, are the poorest in our society. They are more likely to have a fire in their home and they are less likely to be insured.

The fire service has a key role in the promotion of fire safety to encourage safe behaviour in all sections of our community and to work to reduce the incidents of arson.

Q36. Most fires which lead to death or injury occur in the home.

True
False
Cannot say

Answer [ ]

Q37. Arson is on the increase.

True
False
Cannot say

Answer [ ]

Q38. The poorest in our community are more likely to deliberately start fires.

True
False
Cannot say

Answer [ ]

Q39. The only role of the fire service is to put out fires.

True
False
Cannot say

Answer [ ]

Turn over the page.

Q40. We can be proud of our fire service.

True
False
Cannot say

Answer [   ]

End of the test.

5

Interview and team exercise, physical tests and references

Congratulations if you are reading this chapter having been notified that you have passed the written tests and are invited to attend the next stage of the recruitment process. You have succeeded where many other very good candidates have failed.

Allow yourself a day or two while you enjoy your achievement but then put aside any sense of pride and start to take very seriously the next challenge. In a few weeks' time or possibly sooner you must demonstrate that you are very well suited to the role of firefighter. There will be a lot of other candidates who will be trying to do the same and there will not be enough positions for all of you. The recruiters will have to make some difficult decisions and will have to choose between candidates on the basis of what you say and how well you represent yourself on the day.

You may well find that on the same day you must undertake some work-related exercise or additional physical exercises, in which case you must prepare for the interview whilst maintaining your level of fitness through appropriate exercise.

It is possible that with the invitation you receive a supplementary application form which you must complete and return.

The interview

Do not be even a second late and dress in a very smart business-like manner. Firefighters are in a uniformed service and you need to look and act the part.

You are likely to be interviewed by more than one person. They may take it in turns to ask questions or one may take the lead on the questions while another takes notes. A serving firefighter may also be present but this is not guaranteed. Instead, the interview could be conducted by professionals in personnel with no direct experience of the Fire Service.

The interview is likely to be highly structured. By this I mean that every candidate is likely to be given the same information and be asked the same questions. At times this may mean that the interview appears rather stilted.

An interview is an oral exam – you are judged on what you say in response to the questions asked. If you are a quiet and reserved person or not really used to talking about yourself or how you feel about things then you will need to get practising.

Start, if it helps, by making written notes on what you want to say but, and this is important, remember that you have to speak your answers and are not allowed to hand in an essay. So memorize your notes if it helps but then put them away and get practising by speaking.

You will not be allowed to make a speech that you have prepared. An interview is a conversation. It could go in a number of directions and you must listen and respond to what the interviewer says. You must learn to be able to adjust your answer in response to the question and make sure that your answer is to the point while sufficiently detailed. You may then be asked follow-up questions based on what you have said in reply to the previous question and again you will have to provide a clear, relevant answer. It is a difficult balance to get right but that is all part of the challenge.

To get good at interviews you have to practise but it is important that you undertake the right sort of practice. Try the following method:

1. Revise what you wrote on your application form – you may be asked a question about it.
2. Start with the information sent with your invitation to attend. It should include an outline of the day and what to expect at interview. The letter may suggest the broad subject areas that will be covered during the interview. If your letter did not indicate the subject areas to be covered in the interview then try these:
    – why you want to be a firefighter;
    – when you have shown commitment, determination and reliability;
    – when you have worked as a part of a team to overcome a difficult, stressful or unpleasant situation;
    – what you understand by equality and community.
3. If you have not already done so, undertake some research by, for example:
    i Visiting your local fire station and asking them if they are willing to show you around the station. Collect a copy of any leaflets on fire safety that are on display and read them.
    ii Researching on the Web the responsibilities and priorities of the Fire Service. Find out about the Service's commitment to equality of opportunity both amongst its staff and in the provision of services to the general public. Think about how such a commitment can be delivered on a day-to-day basis by firefighters.

iii Reading about the Service's efforts to improve the public's knowledge of fire prevention as well as fire fighting. Work out how you think fire prevention could be improved.

iv Visiting your local library to find out more about the community in which you live and the services offered to the young and old and the socially excluded.

v Researching the ethnic minority groups that live in your community, the minority religions and languages spoken.

vi Learning what are the responsibilities of a firefighter the skills they must hold and the knowledge they must acquire.

4. Take the subject areas from point 2 and what you have established from the research described at point 3 and work out what you could say at interview on each subject. Keep reviewing these responses until you are really familiar with them.

5. Now get someone to ask you some of the typical interview questions suggested below and, without looking at any notes, try to answer them. If you have done your research you should be able to provide clear, relevant answers to the questions. If you find it hard to give an answer other than one that is either very brief or very long then you need to go back and review what you want to say until you understand it and can talk about it.

6. Once you start answering these questions with confidence, get your helper to ask the same question in a different way (I have suggested a few alternative ways of asking the same question below). Also, get them to start asking follow-up questions so that you have to think on your feet and adjust your answers (some follow-up questions have also been suggested).

7. Keep practising under these sorts of realistic interview situations until, despite feeling nervous on the day, you can talk

confidently and clearly about yourself, the responsibilities of a firefighter, your community and equal opportunities.

Try making a video recording of yourself and playing it back to see for yourself how well you are doing.

Typical interview questions and follow-up questions

You cannot rely on the interview being structured in the way suggested here, nor can you assume that the questions will be the same as the examples here. This is why it is so important that you know your subject and practise talking about it in a variety of ways. That way you can be prepared for the question.

To assist you in your practice try these typical questions:

1. Why do you want to be a firefighter?

Other ways this question might be asked:
Q. What experience can you bring to the role of firefighter?
Q. What have you done that qualifies you to be a firefighter?
Q. Which of your qualities makes you most suitable for the role of firefighter?

2. Describe a situation where you have motivated others to achieve something difficult.

Possible follow-up question:
Q. How did you feel about the outcome of this?

3. When have you worked as a team to resolve a problem?

Possible follow-up question:
Q. How did you inform your supervisor of this situation?

4. Why do you think equality of opportunity is important to the Fire Service?

Possible follow-up question:
Q. Can you think of any other reason why equality of opportunity is important?

5. Tell me about an occasion when you have had to deal with a stressful situation and how you coped with it.

Possible follow-up question:
Q. How could you have done things better?

6. Tell me about something you have done that demonstrates commitment.

7. We live in a multicultural society. Do you think this brings any advantages and, if so, what are they?

Possible follow-up question:
Q. Can you think of any other advantages?

8. Describe to me a situation when you have explained something to a group of people.

Possible follow-up question:
Q. How would you have dealt with this situation if one of the group could not speak English or was hearing impaired?

9. Tell me about a situation where you have had to deal with someone distressed or upset and tell me how you managed it.

Possible follow-up question:
Q. What else might you have done?

10. Why do you think community knowledge is important to the Fire Service?

Team exercises

Some Authorities used these exercises, alongside interviews, as an additional tool to select between candidates. Their use is on the increase and I suspect more Authorities will begin to use them.

They involve you sitting with a group of other candidates and being observed and even video taped while you discuss a number of Fire Service-related topics.

These exercises can be organized in a number of ways, but in general they involve each candidate being given a different topic to introduce into the discussion and having a few minutes to decide what to say on the subject.

The candidates take it in turns to introduce their subject and open it up for discussion within the group. When it is your subject being discussed you are leading the discussion. When it is the turn of another candidate to introduce their topic and lead the discussion it is your role to listen carefully to their introduction and to make a contribution to the discussion.

In this sort of exercise the assessors are looking for candidates who can:

- have a constructive conversation with people they have not met before;
- listen to the views of others;
- develop a view by incorporating the views of others into the discussion;
- speak confidently and clearly on a subject that is new to them;
- encourage and support others in a conversation.

Useful tips when undertaking a team exercise include:

- When it is your turn to lead the exercise, introduce yourself by name.

- Tell your group what subject you are going to introduce.
- Explain that you are going to make a few brief points on the subject and then open it up for discussion.
- Make your few (ie two) brief points, making sure that you speak clearly and with confidence.
- Then invite other members of the group to contribute.
- If any member of the group has not had the chance to speak then respectfully invite them to make a contribution.
- If someone makes a point with which you agree, tell them so.

When it is your turn to hear someone else's introduction to a subject, listen carefully to what they say and when an opportunity presents itself offer some additional contribution to the subject.

Make eye contact with someone when you speak to them. Do not enter into a heated disagreement with another member of your group and if other members of your group start arguing then gently intervene in an attempt to resolve the conflict.

Physical tests

At one or more points in the recruitment process you will face a series of fitness tests. They are likely to involve tests of both your aerobic fitness and strength. They may also require you to complete fitness tests that involve tasks related to the work of a firefighter (these are called work sample tests). The physical tests many involve any of the following:

Examples of aerobic fitness and strength tests

Back pull
Hand grip
Lung capacity
Running

Examples of work sampled physical tests

Extending a ladder
Climbing stairs
Deploying a hose
Moving through confined spaces with restricted visibility
Exercise while wearing breathing apparatus
Exercise in full firefighting gear

A test administrator will explain to you and may even demonstrate what you have to do in any of these exercises. There will be a minimum standard that you must realize in order to pass.

At the same time as preparing for the written tests and interview you must also practise for the physical tests. These physical exercises together with the written test practice will require a significant commitment from you over a considerable length of time.

Begin straight away a programme of exercise that is as similar as possible to the task on which you will be tested. So, for example, if you have to pass a test that involves running, make sure that your programme involves lots of running. If the test is primarily of your upper body strength then work with weights to build up your strength.

The standard of fitness demanded by the Service is high and you will need to undertake a significant amount of practice over many months if you are to be sure of success. This preparation will serve you well both in the application stage and during your initial firefighter fitness training.

Many people believe they are fitter than in fact they are. Because you used to play a team sport or represent a club in athletics to a high standard when you were younger is no guarantee that you are fit enough now to pass these tests. If you are not currently training then you need to start without delay. Train at least 3 times a week and push yourself during these sessions. Depending on your starting point, it could take many weeks or months before you realize the correct standard of fitness.

Get professional advice

Fitness advisers are available at all fitness clubs and will help you to devise a suitable fitness programme to suit your circumstances. Explain that you face the Firefighter fitness test – take along any description of the physical test that has been sent to you.

If it is some time since you have undertaken strenuous physical exercise then consider making an appointment with your GP. Explain what you intend to do and ask if there is any reason why you should not begin such a programme.

If close to your test you sustain an injury or are unwell and this will adversely affect your ability in the test, then contact the recruitment team in the Fire Authority and explain the problem. They may agree to you attending on another day but are likely to require a doctor's note confirming that the reason is genuine.

Medicals

Towards the end of the application process, if you have passed all the stages to that point you will be asked to undertake a medical examination. Certain medical conditions are considered incompatible with the role of firefighter. Examples include poor eyesight and asthma. It is understandably a great disappointment for any candidate who, having passed so many hurdles in the recruitment process, then fails at almost the final stage.

If you know of any reason or have any condition that may mean that you might fail the medical, it is probably best to make enquiries before you progress too far down the recruitment process and possibly save yourself the trouble of applying and attending for test, interview and so on only to be rejected on health grounds.

Ask the Authority's recruitment team whether or not your condition could be an issue. Your GP may be able to provide some indication of whether or not your health may exclude you from the Service but note that while this may be a useful indicator, only the Fire Authority doctor can say for certain. By asking in advance at least you will be forewarned of a potential problem.

Some candidates arrange for a private eyesight test. Once they have a positive result they can then be sure that they can progress with their application in the knowledge that their eyesight will not let them down at the medical.

References

With your prior consent a number of references will be taken and checks made. This will occur at various stages of the application process and may include:

- references from your employment or study going back some years;
- a check to confirm you have a right to work in the UK;
- a police record check to confirm that you have declared any criminal convictions;
- references confirming any community or voluntary work.

Be sure that you detail accurately the names and addresses, including post code, of all referees. Omissions or errors can lead to significant delays and can prevent you from starting employment with the Service until satisfactory replies have been obtained. It is well worth writing to or calling your referees, asking permission to use them and explaining who might contact them. Take this opportunity to stress how important it is that they kindly reply as soon as is convenient.

Many applicants fear that they do not have anyone suitable as a referee. This is perhaps because they have moved between jobs or not had paid work for some time or have been self-employed.

If one of these situations applies to you then you will need to do a bit more work than someone who has been in the same job since school or college, but otherwise there is no reason why you should not be able to provide acceptable references.

Consider approaching the Fire Authority Recruitment Team for guidance. Briefly describe your situation and ask, given your circumstance, who they recommend would be best to approach for a reference.

Take care to disclose any periods of unemployment or long holidays and if you are unemployed give serious thought to undertaking some unpaid community or voluntary work. It will mean that you update your skills and should provide a reference.

If you are self-employed or a subcontractor then it may be acceptable if you provide as referees a number of your recent customers.

If you have moved between lots of jobs then start straight away, contacting each employer seeking permission to use them as a referee and obtaining their full postal address. Explain what you are hoping to do and how important it is to you and that you are sorry to have to trouble them. They may be willing to confirm dates of employment and any other relevant details of which you are unsure.

What to do if you fail at interview

It is a considerable disappointment to fail at interview when you have succeeded in getting so far along the recruitment process and worked so hard to try to realize your ambition to become a firefighter.

To start again and reapply at the next call for applicants means that you will again have to pass the application form sift, written tests and physical fitness tests before you again have the opportunity to pass at interview.

The prospect of reapplying will be a serious test of your character and will require you to show considerable determination and commitment. You will be one among many very good candidates who fail at interview. If you find the resolve to reapply then you may succeed in your next attempt. It is common for successful applicants to have succeeded only after the sixth or more attempts.

You will get better at interview through the experience of being interviewed and by preparing for each interview.

If you really want to become a firefighter then you have no alternative but to try and try again.

Ask the Authority to tell you where you went wrong. Go over your interview and try to work out how you could do better. Keep researching the role of the Fire Service and the community in which you live. Make sure that you appreciate the importance of the Service's equal opportunities policy and understand it and how it might be applied in a practical way. Ensure that you understand the value that the Service places on a diverse workforce and serving all sections of community.

If you feel that you may have strayed off the point on a number of occasions or not provided sufficient detail in your answers, then practise more at answering example questions in a mock interview-type situation.

I wish you every success with your next application.

6

Answers and explanations

Chapter 3, Written tests and practice questions

Understanding information

Passage 1

Q1. Answer False.
Explanation The passage reported that the trainee was wearing a firefighter's protective suit, boots and helmet.

Q2. Answer Cannot say.
Explanation The passage states that the fire was in a room which could be on board a ship or on land.

Q3. Answer True.

Q4. Answer True.

Q5. Answer False.
Explanation The passage said that the centre was in Gosport.

Q6. Answer Cannot say.
     Explanation The passage states that poorly maintained
     electrical equipment and deposits of oil and grease are
     most likely to cause a fire on a ship. You cannot tell from
     the given information whether it is electrical equipment
     or oil and grease that causes the most fires.

Q7. Answer True.

Q8. Answer Cannot say.
     Explanation The passage does not provide any advice on
     this subject.

Q9. Answer True.

Q10. Answer Cannot say.
     Explanation Whilst most people may agree with this
     statement, the passage does not comment on this issue so
     you cannot answer it from the information provided.

Passage 2

Q11. Answer False.
     Explanation The passage states that there are often many
     aerosol cans on boats.

Q12. Answer False
     Explanation The trainees had first-hand experience of
     foam, dry powder and carbon dioxide extinguishers.

Q13. Answer True.

Q14. Answer False.

Q15. Answer True.

Q16. Answer False.
     Explanation The passage contains no reference to the
     effects of smoke.

Q17. Answer Cannot say.
    Explanation The previous passage commented on the content of the course and this information cannot be used in the following passage.

Q18. Answer Cannot say.
    Explanation The passage makes no comment on the applications of a foam-filled extinguisher.

Q19. Answer True.
    Explanation The passage states that the flame can travel at 5 metres per second and 7 × 5 = 35 which is further than 25 metres.

Q20. Answer Cannot say.
    Explanation The passage does not comment on the qualities of foam extinguishers.

Passage 3

Q21. Answer True.
    Explanation The passage states that this is one of the items that a fire emergency plan should cover.

Q22. Answer True.

Q23. Answer True.

Q24. Answer False.
    Explanation The passage does not make any specific statement that a fire alarm must be fitted.

Q25. Answer False.
    Explanation A fire emergency plan would cover the possibility of an electrical fault but this is not the point of the passage.

Passage 4

Q26. Answer True.

Q27. Answer Cannot say.
Explanation The passage contains no reference to this subject.

Q28. Answer Cannot say.
Explanation Again the passage does not comment on what people should do once evacuated.

Q29. Answer False.
Explanation The passage makes no reference to fire wardens so the statement is false.

Q30. Answer True.
Explanation It is clear from the passage that on discovery of a fire you should raise the alarm and assist in the evacuation of people before considering fighting a fire.

Passage 5

Q31. Answer True.
Explanation The passage states that when tackling a fire you should position yourself between the fire and the way out. When fighting the fire you will be facing it so it is likely that your back will be facing your exit.

Q32. Answer True.
Explanation Class A fires are stated to be solid objects and a table is a solid object.

Q33. Answer True.

Q34. Answer False.
Explanation The passage only refers to places of work and not homes.

Q35. Answer False.
Explanation The passage describes which extinguisher to use on type A, B and C fires but does not state the advantages of the various types.

Passage 6

Q36. Answer True.

Q37. Answer False.
Explanation The passage states that smoke and fire can incapacitate people as the fire spreads. They need not be trapped for this danger to exist.

Q38. Answer Cannot tell.
Explanation This passage does not comment on the provision of firefighting equipment or training in its use.

Q39. Answer Cannot tell.
Explanation The passage makes no reference to smoke alarms.

Q40. Answer True.

Passage 7

Q41. Answer False.
Explanation The passage states that all three are needed for a fire to occur, not that if all three are present a fire will occur.

Q42. Answer False.
Explanation The passage states that oxygen is also found in a chemical form.

Q43. Answer True.

Q44. Answer Cannot tell.
Explanation The passage does not range the examples in terms of flammability.

Q45. Answer True.

Passage 8

Q46. Answer True.

Q47. Answer True.
Explanation This is clearly stated in the last sentence of the passage.

Q48. Answer False.
Explanation The passage makes no comment on this issue.

Q49. Answer False.
Explanation It is stated in the passage that an assessment might also require an assessment of whether or not the risks are acceptable and if anything can be done to reduce them.

Q50. Answer True.

Verbal reasoning

Verbal reasoning question type 1

Q1. Answer A.
Explanation A boat can be powered by sails and a car by its engine.

Q2. Answer B.
Explanation One of the products of fire is smoke and words can be used to produce sentences.

Q3. Answer D.
Explanation A river runs to the sea and a telephone is connected to an exchange.

Q4. Answer B.
Explanation Smooth is the opposite to fuzzy, and interior is the opposite to surface.

Q5. Answer B.
Explanation You can be jailed for the crime of fraud and expelled from school for smoking.

Q6. Answer A.
Explanation A swan is a type of bird and a mechanical engineer is one of the specialists in that profession.

Q7. Answer C.
Explanation Polish can be described as waxy and baby food as mushy.

Q8. Answer C
Explanation Height and weight are two forms of measurement and joyous and sombre are two types of sentiment.

Q9. Answer D.
Explanation To guess is to estimate something and to inflate something is to expand it.

Q10. Answer B.
Explanation Stupid is the opposite of sensible and transparent is the opposite of opaque.

Q11. Answer A.
Explanation A book is made of pages and a cloth is made of yarns (both pages and yarns are made of fibres).

Q12. Answer D.
Explanation In order to be operated a violin needs a bow and a lock a key.

Q13. Answer C.
Explanation Barley is a type of cereal and Parliament is a type of Assembly.

Q14. Answer C.
Explanation Photosynthesis requires sunlight and a concert requires an orchestra.

Q15. Answer C.
Explanation Acid and alkali are opposites and strict is the opposite to lax.

Q16. Answer B.
Explanation Languages are used to communicate and a microscope to magnify.

Q17. Answer D.
Explanation Both pairs of words have similar meanings.

Q18. Answer C.
Explanation Proponent and supporter mean the same, as does myth and story.

Q19. Answer A.
Explanation Hockey is a type of ballgame and a painkiller is a type of medicine.

Q20. Answer D.
Explanation Both pairs of words are opposites.

Q21. Answer B.
Explanation Geology is a branch of science and statistics a branch of mathematics.

Q22. Answer C.
Explanation A set square and a ruler are instruments used in geometry and an oblong and cuboid are types of shape in geometry.

Q23. Answer A.
Explanation Refuse is another way of saying decline and dilute is an alternative way to describe weakening something.

Q24. Answer D.
Explanation Construction and transportation are both types of industry and turtles and lizards are two types of reptile.

Q25. Answer A
Explanation Flyover and viaduct are types of bridge and Archbishop and Ayatollah are two types of religious leader.

Verbal reasoning question type 2

Q1.   Answer 4 (closest in meaning).
Q2.   Answer 3 (opposite).
Q3.   Answer 1 (closest in meaning).
Q4.   Answer 2 (closest in meaning).
Q5.   Answer 4 (opposite).
Q6.   Answer 1 (closest in meaning).
Q7.   Answer 3 (closest in meaning).
Q8.   Answer 3 (closest in meaning).
Q9.   Answer 2 (closest in meaning).
Q10. Answer 1 (closest in meaning).
Q11. Answer 2 (opposite).
Q12. Answer 4 (closest in meaning).
Q13. Answer 1 (opposite).
Q14. Answer 4 (opposite).
Q15. Answer 2 (closest in meaning).
Q16. Answer 3 (closest in meaning).
Q17. Answer 3 (opposite).
Q18. Answer 1 (opposite).
Q19. Answer 4 (closest in meaning).
Q20. Answer 4 (opposite).

Using numbers

Revise the basics
Addition
Q1.   Answer 10.
Q2.   Answer 15.
Q3.   Answer 13.
Q4.   Answer 12.

Q5.   Answer 14.
Q6.   Answer 13.
Q7.   Answer 12.
Q8.   Answer 10.
Q9.   Answer 13.
Q10. Answer 11.
Q11. Answer 23.
Q12. Answer 27.
Q13. Answer 31.
Q14. Answer 25.
Q15. Answer 33.
Q16. Answer 30.
Q17. Answer 32.
Q18. Answer 36.
Q19. Answer 31.
Q20. Answer 39.
Q21. Answer 689.
Q22. Answer 859.
Q23. Answer 999.
Q24. Answer 634.
Q25. Answer 931.
Q26. Answer 872.
Q27. Answer 960.
Q28. Answer 1,493.
Q29. Answer 1,142.
Q30. Answer 1,711.

Sums that relate to the calculation of time
Q31. Answer 57 minutes.
Q32. Answer 1 hour 54 minutes.
Q33. Answer 44 minutes.
Q34. Answer 1 hour 55 minutes.
Q35. Answer 1 hour 20 minutes.
Q36. Answer 1 hour 46 minutes.
Q37. Answer 1 hour.

Q38. Answer 1 hour and 39 minutes.
Q39. Answer 2 hours and 56 minutes.
Q40. Answer 2 hours and 43 minutes.
Q41. Answer 2 hours and 26 minutes.
Q42. Answer 3 hours and 3 minutes.
Q43. Answer 3 hours and 11 minutes.
Q44. Answer 4 hours and 50 minutes.
Q45. Answer 7 hours and 24 minutes.
Q46. Answer 5 hours and 28 minutes.
Q47. Answer 10 hours and 59 minutes.
Q48. Answer 7 hours.
Q49. Answer 12 hours and 7 minutes.
Q50. Answer 9 hours and 12 minutes.

Subtraction
Q1.   Answer 1.
Q2.   Answer 6.
Q3.   Answer 7.
Q4.   Answer 8.
Q5.   Answer 6.
Q6.   Answer 8.
Q7.   Answer 8.
Q8.   Answer 12.
Q9.   Answer 9.
Q10. Answer 13.
Q11. Answer 113.
Q12. Answer 160.
Q13. Answer 241.
Q14. Answer 691.
Q15. Answer 213.
Q16. Answer 149.
Q17. Answer 150.
Q18. Answer 536.
Q19. Answer 91.
Q20. Answer 187.

Q21. Answer 49.
Q22. Answer 275.
Q23. Answer 249.
Q24. Answer 195.
Q25. Answer 368.
Q26. Answer 437.
Q27. Answer 335.
Q28. Answer 138.
Q29. Answer 414.
Q30. Answer 89.

More sums that relate to the calculation of time
Q1.   Answer 28 minutes.
Q2.   Answer 14 minutes.
Q3.   Answer 7 minutes.
Q4.   Answer 13 minutes.
Q5.   Answer 6 minutes.
Q6.   Answer 1 hour 13 minutes.
Q7.   Answer 48 minutes.
Q8.   Answer 51 minutes.
Q9.   Answer 38 minutes.
Q10. Answer 33 minutes.
Q11. Answer 38 minutes.
Q12. Answer 1 hour 22 minutes.
Q13. Answer 53 minutes.
Q14. Answer 14 minutes.
Q15. Answer 55 minutes.
Q16. Answer 25 minutes.
Q17. Answer 3 hours 14 minutes.
Q18. Answer 25 minutes.
Q19. Answer 3 hours 34 minutes.
Q20. Answer 4 minutes.
Q21. Answer 3 hours 11 minutes.

Multiplication
Q1. Answer 30.
Q2. Answer 18.
Q3. Answer 32.
Q4. Answer 18.
Q5. Answer 36.
Q6. Answer 16.
Q7. Answer 21.
Q8. Answer 35.
Q9. Answer 27.
Q10. Answer 48.
Q11. Answer 32.
Q12. Answer 36.
Q13. Answer 55.
Q14. Answer 42.
Q15. Answer 49.
Q16. Answer 56.
Q17. Answer 54.
Q18. Answer 63.
Q19. Answer 72.
Q20. Answer 88.

Division and percentages
Q1. Answer 4.
Q2. Answer 12.5.
Q3. Answer 7.
Q4. Answer 9.
Q5. Answer 9.
Q6. Answer 5.
Q7. Answer 3.
Q8. Answer 9.
Q9. Answer 12.
Q10. Answer 9.
Q11. Answer 21.
Q12. Answer 15.

Q13. Answer 2.5.
Q14. Answer 15.
Q15. Answer 21.
Q16. Answer 25.
Q17. Answer 12.
Q18. Answer 2.5.
Q19. Answer 240.
Q20. Answer 72.

Using numbers and time
Situation 1

Q1.   Answer 26 minutes.

Q2.   Answer 26 minutes.
       Explanation 41 minutes have passed from the time of the
       call to now, which leaves 26 minutes.

Q3.   Answer 6 minutes.
Q4.   Answer 10 minutes.
Q5.   Answer 12 minutes.
Q6.   Answer 10 minutes.
Q7.   Answer 55 minutes.
Q8.   Answer 24 minutes.
Q9.   Answer 8 minutes.
Q10. Answer 1 minute.
Q11. Answer 13 minutes.
Q12. Answer 20 minutes.
Q13. Answer 19 minutes.
Q14. Answer 15 minutes.
Q15. Answer 19 minutes.

More using numbers and time
Situation 2
Q1.   Answer 55 minutes
       Explanation The crew left the station at 09.00 and took
       15 minutes to reach the incident. They arrived at the
       incident therefore at 09.15. The time now is 10.10 so
       they have so far been at the incident for 55 minutes.

Q2.   Answer 50 minutes.
Q3.   Answer 93 minutes.
Q4.   Answer 18 minutes.
Q5.   Answer 32 minutes.
Q6.   Answer 64 minutes.
Q7.   Answer 68 minutes.
Q8.   Answer 15 minutes.
Q9.   Answer 28 minutes.
Q10.   Answer 66 minutes.
Q11.   Answer 44 minutes.
Q12.   Answer 25 minutes.
Q13.   Answer 74 minutes.
Q14.   Answer 1 minute.
Q15.   Answer 67 minutes.

Even more using numbers and time
Situation 3
Q1.   Answer 44 minutes.
Q2.   Answer 6 minutes.
Q3.   Answer 15 minutes.
Q4.   Answer 25 minutes.
Q5.   Answer 34 minutes.
Q6.   Answer 22 minutes.
Q7.   Answer 6 minutes.
Q8.   Answer 13 minutes.
Q9.   Answer 65 minutes.

Q10. Answer 20 minutes.
Q11. Answer 16 minutes.
Q12. Answer none – time has run out.
Q13. Answer 30 minutes.
Q14. Answer 87 minutes.
Q15. Answer 9 minutes.

Numerical reasoning

Sequencing

Q1. Answer C.
      Explanation The series is the sequence of even numbers.

Q2. Answer B.
      Explanation It is the sequence of odd numbers starting with 101.

Q3. Answer D.
      Explanation The last term is doubled each move.

Q4. Answer B.
      Explanation 3 is added each move in the series.

Q5. Answer A.
      Explanation It is the sequence of the 5 times table starting with 6 × 5.

Q6. Answer B.
      Explanation You subtract 7 each time.

Q7. Answer C.
      Explanation The sequence is the 4 times table starting with 8 × 4 = 32.

Q8. Answer D.
      Explanation –17 each move in the sequence.

Q9. Answer A.
      Explanation The sequence involves trebling the last term, eg 5 × 3 = 15, 15 × 3 = 45.

Q10. Answer D.
Explanation The sequence involves adding together the previous two terms, eg 12 + 14 = 26.

Q11. Answer B.
Explanation The sequence is the 8 times table starting with 5 × 8 = 40.

Q12. Answer C.
Explanation The sequence is the 4 times table starting with 4 × 14 = 56.

Q13. Answer B.
Explanation Each step involves adding 48 to the previous sum.

Q14. Answer C.
Explanation 3 is added each move in the sequence, for example (−14 + 3 = −11).

Q15. Answer A.
Explanation At each step in the sequence 4.5 is added to the previous amount.

Q16. Answer D.
Explanation Minus 12.5 each step.

Q17. Answer A.
Explanation The previous sum is doubled each step and then one is added, eg 6 + 6 + 1 = 13.

Q18. Answer C.
Explanation The sequence is the 9 times table starting with 9 × 6 = 54.

Q19. Answer B.
Explanation Minus 200 each step.

Q20. Answer C.
Explanation 6 is added to the previous sum each step.

Q21. Answer B.
Explanation The previous amount is multiplied by 5.

Q22. Answer D.
Explanation Add 9 each step.

Q23. Answer A.
Explanation 10.5 is added each step.

Q24. Answer C.
Explanation Minus 17 each step.

Q25. Answer D.
Explanation Divide the previous sum by 3.

Q26. Answer C.
Explanation 17 is added each step.

Q27. Answer A.
Explanation Triple each previous sum then –1.

Q28. Answer B.
Explanation The sequence is the 7 times table starting with $7 \times 7 = 49$.

Q29. Answer D.
Explanation Add the previous two terms to get the next value in the sequence.

Q30. Answer A.
Explanation The sequence is the sum of the 12 times table starting with 12×12.

Non-verbal reasoning

Question type 1
Q1. Answer B.
Explanation Shape B also has three spots.

Q2.   Answer C.
Explanation Each question shape is divided into two equal parts horizontally.

Q3.   Answer B.
Explanation The question shapes and suggested Answer B are all made from 12 crosses.

Q4.   Answer C.
Explanation The question shapes have shaded circles at both ends as does C.

Q5.   Answer C.
Explanation The question shapes have arrows going in opposite directions as does C.

Q6.   Answer A.
Explanation Both question shapes comprise even numbers of squares as does shape A.

Q7.   Answer A.
Explanation Both question shapes and A are three-dimensional shapes.

Q8.   Answer C.
Explanation The question shapes and C are isosceles triangles.

Q9.   Answer A.
Explanation The question shapes contain 3 triangles, 3 circles and 2 squares; only shape A has this configuration.

Q10. Answer A.
Explanation The question shapes are made from four triangles; only A has this quality.

Q11. Answer C.
Explanation The question circles comprise six uneven segments, one of which is shaded. C shares these characteristics (A does not as its segments are regular).

Q12. Answer B.
Explanation Both question shapes are 3-dimensional with both flat and curved surfaces. These qualities are shared with shape B.

Q13. Answer C.
Explanation The bar charts represent a total value of 6, as does question shape C.

Q14. Answer B.
Explanation The shape is rotated but identical in both question shapes and B.

Q15. Answer A.
Explanation The number and length of arrows is shared by the question shapes and question shape A.

Q16. Answer C.
Explanation The common relationship is that the number of triangles is odd and the majority are shaded.

Q17. Answer A.
Explanation The question shapes and A all have two triangles both either inside or outside a circle.

Q18. Answer A.
Explanation The question shapes and A comprise 3 triangles, 5 squares (4 of which are shaded) and 1 circle.

Q19. Answer C.
Explanation The shapes are moving in a clockwise direction around the four squares that make up the question shapes. C would be the shape that follows the two question shapes.

Q20. Answer C.
Explanation The question shapes include a sequence of shapes that runs diamond, square, circle, triangle. This sequence is found only in the question shapes and shape C.

Question type 2

Q21. Answer C.
Explanation The outer circle is moving consistently around the outside of the large circle.

Q22. Answer B.
Explanation The square turns into a triangle and then back into a square and the arrow direction alternates.

Q23. Answer A.
Explanation The shaded area is rotating clockwise, obscuring the shapes below.

Q24. Answer A.
Explanation The sequence is first squares and circles then all circles followed by squares and circles again and then all squares.

Q25. Answer B.
Explanation The outer circles are transformed into spikes, one each step in the sequence in an anticlockwise direction starting from the bottom left.

Q26. Answer A.
Explanation The number of shaded squares is decreasing by three each step.

Q27. Answer C.
Explanation One shape is removed each step and the direction of the shading is moving around the shapes in a clockwise direction.

Q28. Answer B.
Explanation The number of shaded circles increases by one each move in the series while the number of crosses decreases and the direction of the diagonal arrows alternates.

Q29. Answer A.
Explanation A circle changes into two arrow heads at each move in the sequence and the direction of the arrows alternates.

Q30. Answer A.
Explanation The 'L' shape is rotating and the diamond changes into a square and back again.

Q31. Answer C.
Explanation The 'L' shape is rotating around the other two fixed shapes in an anticlockwise direction.

Q32. Answer C.
Explanation The empty segment is rotating around and covering the shapes in the segments below.

Q33. Answer B.
Explanation Four triangles become one square each step in the series.

Q34. Answer B.
Explanation At each stage shapes are transformed. The changes start with the squares (which become circles) and when these have all been transformed then it is the turn of the triangles which become diamonds.

Q35. Answer A.
Explanation The series counts down 3, 2, 1 and then starts again.

Q36. Answer B.
Explanation The crosses represent the 7 times table $7 \times 0 = 0, 7 \times 1 = 7, 7 \times 2 = 14, 7 \times 3 = 21$. The shapes are alternating between squares and hexagons.

Q37. Answer C.
Explanation The number of randomly shaped triangles is increasing by two each stage.

Q38. Answer C.
Explanation Squares are transformed into moons, then circles into triangles, the shading is switching sides and between two and three shaded shapes.

Q39. Answer A.
Explanation The wavy lines are decreasing by two each step, and the lines are increasing by three each step starting with nine.

Q40. Answer B.
Explanation The total number of sides on each set of shapes is increasing by five each step.

Chapter 4, Practice tests

Practice test 1

Passage 1
Q1. Answer False.
Explanation The passage states that some businesses may not recover not that a business is unlikely to recover.

Q2. Answer True.
Explanation The passage states that fire may grow unexpectedly fast.

Q3.   Answer True.
       Explanation The passage states that the potential for an
       accidental fire exists in a large number of everyday activ-
       ities including driving a car.

Q4.   Answer Cannot say.
       Explanation The passage makes no reference to this issue
       so the answer must be cannot say.

Q5.   Answer False.
       Explanation The passage states that every year people are
       killed, and even more are injured, by fires that occur in
       the workplace, whilst travelling and in the home.

Passage 2

Q6.   Answer True.
       Explanation The passage also makes a business case for
       taking such precautions.

Q7.   Answer True.
       Explanation The passage states that simple precautions
       could save a business from having to face the devastating
       effects of an accidental fire.

Q8.   Answer False.
       Explanation The passage states that the law compels
       most employers to provide adequate training not all
       employers.

Q9.   Answer True.
       Explanation The passage states that their workforce is
       trained to the very highest standards.

Q10.   Answer Cannot say.
       Explanation The passage makes no comment on this
       issue so you must conclude that you cannot say.

Passage 3

Q11. Answer Cannot say.

Explanation The passage states only that many fires start at night not that more start at night.

Q12. Answer True.

Explanation The truth of this statement can be inferred from the passage which says that all electric appliances not designed to be on all the time should be switched off and unplugged and at a later point in the passage describes washing machines as appliances not designed to be on all the time.

Q13. Answer True.

Explanation The passage states that if you have an open fire always use a spark guard.

Q14. Answer False.

Explanation The passage states that everyone should have a fire safety routine.

Q15. Answer True.

Explanation The statement is another way of saying that you should 'close all doors throughout your property as this will slow down the spread of any heat or smoke generated by a fire'.

Passage 4

Q16. Answer Cannot say.

Explanation The passage states that some supermarkets sell smoke alarms but does not say that they are cheapest in this type of store.

Q17. Answer False.

Explanation The passage states that ideally you should fit them in every room except the bedroom.

Q18. Answer False.
Explanation The passage does not contain any comment about vacuuming a smoke alarm once a year, only from time to time.

Q19. Answer True.
Explanation The passage describes special smoke alarms for people who have difficulty hearing and this is a disability.

Q20. Answer True.
Explanation This is an accurate summary of the passage which states in the opening sentence that fitting a smoke alarm could save lives.

Passage 5

Q21. Answer True.
Explanation The passage states that the findings (ie conclusions) of a fire risk assessment must be recorded.

Q22. Answer False.
Explanation The passage states that most employers are required by law to do this.

Q23. Answer True.
Explanation The passage states that a Fire Safety Inspecting Officer can inhibit the use of a part or all of a building with immediate effect if she or he thinks it is unsafe, and inhibit means stop.

Q24. Answer Cannot say.
Explanation The passage does not comment on the Authorities' attitude to prosecution.

Q25. Answer False.
Explanation The passage states that Local Fire Authorities are responsible for the supervision and enforcement of the regulations.

Passage 6

Q26. Answer Cannot tell.

Explanation There is insufficient information provided to tell if the statement is true or false. This is because if no one slept above the first floor or below ground then the hotel would not require a certificate.

Q27. Answer False.

Explanation The passage states that more than 20 people must work (at any one time) for a certificate to be required.

Q28. Answer True.

Explanation The passage states that any site at which explosive or highly flammable material is stored must also obtain a fire certificate.

Q29. Answer Cannot tell.

Explanation The passage states that if more than 20 work at a location all at the same time then a certificate is required. In the situation described it is not known how many work in the shop at any one time.

Q30. Answer False.

Explanation The passage states that as well as complying with the fire regulations some premises also require a fire certificate. This implies that any employer who has a fire certificate must also comply with the fire regulations.

Practice test 2

Using numbers and time

Q1.   Answer 11.21.
Q2.   Answer 01.24.
Q3.   Answer 03.34.
Q4.   Answer 10.16.
Q5.   Answer 05.30.

Q6.   Answer 77 minutes
       Explanation 1 hour 17 minutes = 60 + 17 = 77 minutes.

Q7.   Answer 6.
       Explanation 24 divided by 4 = 6.

Q8.   Answer 03.33.
       Explanation You have to minus 50 from 04.23. Starting
       with the minutes 50 – 23 brings us to 4.00 and leaves 27
       minutes. 60 – 27 = 33 so the response began at 03.33.

Q9.   Answer 700.
       Explanation 2,100 divided by 3 = 700.

Q10.   Answer 32 minutes.
       Explanation 09.41 is 19 minutes before 10.00 so 19 + 13
       (the time now is 10.13) = 32 minutes.

Q11.   Answer 39.
       Explanation 320 – 281 = 39.

Q12.   Answer 28 minutes.

Q13.   Answer 6.
       Explanation 30 divided by 5 = 6.

Q14.   Answer 14.29.

Q15.   Answer 27.
       Explanation 9 × 3 = 27.

Q16.   Answer 01.38.

Q17.   Answer 80.
       Explanation 200 divided by 5 × 2 = 80.

Q18.   Answer 200.
       Explanation 3 × 60 = 180 + 20 = 200.

Q19.   Answer 310.
       Explanation 297 + 13 = 310.

Q20. Answer 46 minutes.

Q21. Answer 70.
Explanation 280 divided by 4 = 70.

Q22. Answer 12.05.
Explanation You have to minus 70 from 01.15. Minus 15 brings us to 01.00 and leaves 55 minutes, 60 – 55 = 05, so the response began at 12.05.

Q23. Answer 36 km.
Explanation 2 × 3 × 6 = 36.

Q24. Answer 52 minutes.

Q25. Answer 44 hours.
Explanation 100 – 12 = 88.   50 × $^{88}/_{100}$ = 44.

Practice test 3

Verbal reasoning

Type 1

Q1. Answer 2.
Explanation The pairs are examples of types of thing. Tabloid and Broadsheet are types of newspaper and Spanish and Hindi are types of language.

Q2. Answer 4.
Explanation Both pairs comprise an item and a product of it. Candles produce light and waves produce surf.

Q3. Answer 1.
Explanation Both pairs describe an item and one of its principal components. Furniture can contain wood and a pencil lead is often graphite.

Q4. Answer 4.
Explanation The relationship is one of an item and its effect. Medicine can produce a cure and fire warmth (insulation cannot produce warmth, only help retain it).

Q5. Answer 4.
Explanation The relationship is one of an item and what it is made of. A house is made of bricks and a pension a series of monthly or weekly contributions.

Q6. Answer 3.
Explanation The relationship is that of what potential the item has. A seed can grow into a plant and an inference can lead to a conclusion.

Q7. Answer 4.
Explanation Both pairs are opposites.

Q8. Answer 1.
Explanation The relationship is one of one item making the other possible. Many animals need air to breathe and a solution is only possible if you first have a problem.

Q9. Answer 2.
Explanation Both pairs comprise words with similar meanings.

Q10. Answer 1.
Explanation The relationship is one of an important tool and the activity in which it is used. A pencil is used extensively in art and a phone in telecommunications.

Q11. Answer 3.
Explanation The relationship is the negative effect of something. The sun can burn you and criticism can make you angry.

Q12. Answer 1.
Explanation The relationship is words that sound the same but have different meanings and spellings.

Q13. Answer 2.
Explanation The relationship is one of potential. Music has the potential to please and research to make discoveries.

Q14. Answer 1.
Explanation The pairs are opposites.

Type 2
Q15. Answer 2.

Q16. Answer 3.
Explanation Ignore means the opposite of investigate.

Q17. Answer 1.

Q18. Answer 3.
Explanation Remain means the opposite of escape.

Q19. Answer 4.

Q20. Answer 4.
Explanation Negative means the opposite of affirmative.

Q21. Answer 2.

Q22. Answer 3.
Explanation Consult means the opposite of ignore (if you ignore someone you may insult them but ignore does not mean the same as insult).

Q23. Answer 4.

Q24. Answer 1.

Q25. Answer 2.
Explanation Deluge means the opposite of drought.

Q26. Answer 3.
Explanation Liberate means the opposite of enslave.

Q27. Answer 2.
Explanation Conceal means the opposite of forthright.

Q28. Answer 4.

Q29. Answer 2.

Q30. Answer 1.

Practice test 4

Sequencing

Q1.   Answer 2.
       Explanation Values double each step in the sequence.

Q2.   Answer 3.
       Explanation The sequence is the 9 times table starting with $3 \times 9 = 27$.

Q3.   Answer 1.
       Explanation Doubled the previous sum then – 10 each step to get the new total.

Q4.   Answer 4.
       Explanation Minus 6 each step in the sequence.

Q5.   Answer 2.
       Explanation Minus 13 each step.

Q6.   Answer 3.
       Explanation The rows increase by the same value (row 1 by 3, row 2 by 6, row 3 by 12) and the numbers in the columns double (column 1 3, 6, 12, column 2 6, 12, 24).

Q7.   Answer 4.
       Explanation Rows double, columns increase by constant number (column 1 by 12, column 2 by 24).

Q8.   Answer 2.
       Explanation Rows double, value of columns are halved.

Q9.   Answer 1.
       Explanation Values in rows are increased by constant amount (row 2 by 12, row 3 by 36), columns are multiple of 3 (column 3 $12 \times 3 = 36$, $36 \times 3 = 108$).

Q10.   Answer 3.
       Explanation Rows increase by constant number (row 1 by 15, row 3 by 60), the values in the columns double.

Q11. Answer 4.
   Explanation Rows increase by constant value (row 1 by 10, row 3 by 40), the values in the columns double.

Q12. Answer 2.
   Explanation Rows double, columns decrease by constant value (column 2 decreases by 10, column 3 by 20).

Q13. Answer 2.
   Explanation Values in the rows are halved, columns double.

Q14. Answer 1.
   Explanation Values in rows increase by constant amount (row 1 by 9, row 2 by 18), values in the columns double.

Q15. Answer 4.
   Explanation Values in rows decrease by constant amount (row 2 by 5, row 3 by 2.5), columns divide previous sum by 2.

Q16. Answer 3.
   Explanation Values in rows decrease by constant number (row 1 by 6, row 3 by 44) values in the columns are multiplied by 3.

Q17. Answer 1.
   Explanation The values of rows are multiples of 3, the values of columns increase by constant number (column 2 by 15).

Q18. Answer 4.
   Explanation Values in rows are divided by 3, values of columns decrease by a constant amount (column 1 by 9).

Q19. Answer 2.
   Explanation Rows decrease by constant values (row 3 by 3.5), values of columns are divided by 2.

Q20. Answer 2.
Explanation The values of the rows are doubled, columns decrease by a constant sum (column 2 by 14).

Q21. Answer 1.
Explanation Values in rows are divided by 2, values in columns decrease by constant (column 3 by 1.5).

Q22. Answer 3.
Explanation Add 12 each time.

Q23. Answer 1.
Explanation Add 15.5 each step.

Q24. Answer 3.
Explanation Double the previous sum and minus 2 for the next total.

Q25. Answer 1.
Explanation Minus the previous value each step (−50 − 50 = 0).

Q26. Answer 3.
Explanation Add 14 each step.

Q27. Answer 2.
Explanation Add the previous two values to get the next.

Q28. Answer 4.
Explanation Multiply by 2.5 each step.

Q29. Answer 4.
Explanation Multiply by 4 each step.

Q30. Answer 1.
Explanation Add 16 each step.

Practice test 5

Learning information

Passage 1

Q1.   Answer False.
Explanation The passage states that Southfield is in Newbury.

Q2.   Answer False.
Explanation The appliance is to visit on Sunday.

Q3.   Answer True.
Explanation The passage states that 543 are injured each year.

Q4.   Answer Cannot say.
Explanation The passage states only that the police will be visiting local traders to discourage them from selling fireworks to anyone under the age of 18. From this it cannot be inferred that the traders have actually been doing so.

Q5.   Answer False.
Explanation The passage states that officers and fire-fighters are very concerned that someone could end up hurt, from which it can be inferred that no one has been hurt yet.

Passage 2

Q6.   Answer Cannot say.
Explanation The passage does not say whether the smoke alarms are free.

Q7.   Answer True.
Explanation The passage states that fire stations will be open to the public offering advice on fire and community safety.

Q8.   Answer False.
       Explanation The passage states that the batteries last 10 years.

Q9.   Answer Cannot say.
       Explanation The passage states that wherever possible they will be made fully accessible to people with disabilities but it is not said whether or not it will be possible to make them all accessible.

Q10.   Answer False.
       Explanation The passage states that over 13,000 have been fitted.

Passage 3
Q11.   Answer True.
       Explanation The passage states that over half of the accidental fire deaths in the home were caused by smoking or matches.

Q12.   Answer False.
       Explanation The number of boroughs was three.

Q13.   Answer Cannot say.
       Explanation The passage states that men were more likely than women to be a victim of such an accident and that a higher proportion of deaths occurred in winter. But you cannot infer from this that more men die in the winter months.

Q14.   Answer True.

Q15.   Answer True.

Passage 4
Q16.   Answer False.
       Explanation The passage states that the competition is held every two years.

Q17. Answer True.

Q18. Answer Cannot say.
Explanation The accident involves two cars but the number of dummies is not stated.

Q19. Answer True.

Q20. Answer False.
Explanation The passages states that the competition involves teams of firefighters from all over the country, so it is not international.

Passage 5

Q21. Answer True.
Explanation The passage states that people must realize that they are doing something really quite dangerous.

Q22. Answer Cannot say.
Explanation The passage states that this is the cause of the most common fire in the kitchen but does not say what the most common sort of fire is in general.

Q23. Answer True.
Explanation The passage states that water on the food could cause the oil to explode.

Q24. Answer True.

Q25. Answer True.
Explanation The passage states that the pan should not be more than a third full, which is the same as 33.3 per cent.

Passage 6

Q26. Answer False.
Explanation the passage states that it took three hours, not over three hours.

Q27. Answer True.

Q28. Answer False.
Explanation The passage states that the exercise was held in Bank Station.

Q29. Answer Cannot say.
Explanation The passage makes no mention of this issue.

Q30. Answer True.
Explanation The commissioner's comments support this statement.

Passage 7

Q31. Answer False.
Explanation The passage states that the strategy is for England and Wales.

Q32. Answer True.
Explanation The passage states that they must develop a broader role.

Q33. Answer False.
Explanation It was described as a White Paper.

Q34. Answer Cannot say.
Explanation The reasons for the changes are not mentioned in the passage.

Q35. Answer True.

Passage 8

Q36. Answer True.
Explanation The passage states that the largest single cause of deaths and injuries from fire is accidental fires in the home.

Q37. Answer True.
Explanation The passage states that there is a growing trend in deliberate fires.

Q38. Answer Cannot say.
Explanation The passage states that the poorest in our society are most at risk from deliberately started fires but does not say that they are more likely to start these fires.

Q39. Answer False.
Explanation The passage describes other important roles of the Service.

Q40. Answer Cannot say.
Explanation The passage makes no comment on this issue.

Sources of further information and practice

Sources of information

Web sites
www.firekills-gov.uk/
www.odpm.gov.uk, click on fire
Also visit your local fire station.

Sources of further practice questions

Books

Barrett J and Williams G (2003) *Test Your Own Aptitude*, Kogan Page, London
Tolley H and Thomas K (2000) *How to Pass Numeracy Tests*, Kogan Page, London
Tolley H and Thomas K (2000) *How to Pass Verbal Reasoning Tests*, Kogan Page, London

CD ROMs

Bryon M (Ed) (2002) *Psychometric Tests Volume 1*, The Times Testing Series, Kogan Page, London
Bryon M (Ed) (2002) *Test Your Aptitude Volume 1*, The Times Testing Series, Kogan Page, London